Joanne Wiens's *Simply Sacred:* Stories from School calls us to draw near in much the same way a teacher calls her students to the carpet. As you lean in for the story, you'll encounter images that refuse to sit still on the page to be passively observed. Rather, they wiggle around, shifting position with subtle nuance, as I imagine young students wriggle on the carpet, first choosing this position, then choosing that one in order to see or be seen better. Joanne's tone of gentle grace will lead you into quiet reflection on the Saviour, then nudge you to respond to who he is with how you live. Most beautifully, her words are consistent with her character, which those who've been part of her school can attest to.

—**Arlene Bergen**
Unshaken Ministries

Simply Sacred, the title of the book you now hold, doesn't say the half of it. Joanne Wiens captures here, time after time, phrase after phrase, story after story, the sheer holy beauty hidden among ordinary moments, awkward people, messy circumstances. This book is a riveting testimony of how having eyes to see and ears to hear changes everything, and all of it is told in prose that sings. Buy a dozen: you'll want to give one to every teacher you know, the good ones to encourage them that their work matters, the not-so-good ones to help them wake up.

—**Mark Buchanan**
Author of *God Walk: Moving at the Speed of Your Soul*

Simply Sacred: Stories from School is a delightful and deep book. In each short, readable chapter, Wiens weaves together story, scripture, and theological reflection. Sometimes heartwarming, sometimes heartbreaking, these stories are told with humility and humour, and reflect the author's long service in a Christian school. The book is permeated with a deep love for children and a commitment to the teachable moment. This is an everyday theology forged in the give and take of learning with children with a keen eye to the presence of God in every school day. This will be an excellent resource for teachers, administrators, and anyone who loves children.

—**Carol Penner is Assistant Professor of Theological Studies**
at Conrad Grebel University College.

In *Simply Sacred*, Joanne Wiens opens a window into the world of the Christian school administrator. Within all the hubbub of a K-9 school, Wiens finds reasons to make us laugh, to cry, to wonder, and to find hope. The writer's gift of storytelling, her faith, as well as a keen gift of observation and a love for children, shine through clearly! This book could be required reading for educators looking for inspiration!

—**Victor Winter**
Retired educator/pastor

To the Lessoway family,

SIMPLY
SACRED

STORIES FROM SCHOOL

JOANNE WIENS

FOREWORD BY DR. BERNIE POTVIN

Shalom,

Joanne Wiens

Disclaimer: To protect the identity of individuals, identifying features have been changed or composite stories were used, unless expressed permission was granted.

Printed in Canada

ISBN: 978-1-4866-2229-0
eBook ISBN: 978-1-4866-2230-6

Word Alive Press
119 De Baets Street Winnipeg, MB R2J 3R9
www.wordalivepress.ca

WORD ALIVE
—P R E S S—

MIX
Paper from
responsible sources
FSC
www.fsc.org   FSC® C103567

Cataloguing in Publication information can be obtained from Library and Archives Canada.

In memory of Cora Leffelaar:
friend, office mate, and cheerful greeter
to everyone who entered our school.

CONTENTS

FOREWORD

Recently, a friend asked me to consider taking on a five-month interim position as principal at a little school in southwest Calgary named Menno Simons Christian School. I had recently retired as Associate Dean of Education at a small university in Calgary. I had just completed two very challenging international educational projects—one in Afghanistan and a second in Tanzania. I had lots of reasons not to be a principal in a K-9 school at that time.

However, my friend was persuasive. My decision-making approach was to make a pros-cons list, and the 'pros side' came out on top. I decided that being a school principal would be a walk in the park compared to my previous few years. It might even be fun, one 'last fun run around an education track.' Besides, I had always been attracted to what I understood about Mennonite ways of being in the world, particularly their principles of social justice and community, with Jesus at the centre of everything. I respected my friend. And, I had time on my hands. What could go wrong? I signed on.

My previous two experiences, in schools that laid claim to the adjective 'Christian,' had been more than a little disappointing. My daughter 'learned' that real Christians don't dance, so we don't dance at 'this school.' My son learned that other people could hurt you, but he learned how to hide it as he was being bullied and shoved into lockers. My youngest daughter lasted four weeks with a teacher who didn't care enough about and for her. I once read a bumper sticker that said, 'I feel much better since I gave up hope.' I had just about given up hope and was feeling much better for it, of ever finding someplace actually down that narrow path of the teachings of Jesus, a school in which right relationships trumped being right, and where Jesus was truly at the centre of it all.

But, despite nagging misgivings and my previous disheartening experiences, I signed this five-month contract, hoping for the best (but still secretly expecting the worst). Still, what could go wrong in five months? The question I should have asked, as it turned out, was, 'What would go right?'

I remember my first week as a week of surprises. Warm, genuine welcomes from kids and parents, supportive verbal support offered by teachers, and most surprising of all, that 'feel' we sometimes have, but not often enough, that it was good at this school. I remained suspicious but slowly gave in to the possibility that I had found, not a perfect place, but a good place for me. Here was a school in which right relationships were the reasons for kids and families to be there.

I quickly grew to love this little school. I ended up staying as principal for a year and a half. I had failed retirement but was heading towards a 'pass' in developing a renewed Christian school mindset.

I had work to do as a principal. I joked that this job was going to keep me out of the pool halls and pawn shops. That was a good thing. And part-way through my first year, COVID showed up. Now I was kept out of the discos as well. But despite work and COVID, I practised who I was—one of those curious academic types. I wanted to know more about the school's history. How does a school become 'good?' I found a stack of old school newsletters and began my research. That is where I first came across a name.

Joanne Wiens.

Joanne had been the school principal during its formative years; as I found out later, a main force behind the school's written mission statement—to integrate Christianity into students' lives and experiences. That statement alone impressed me. It felt real, authentic, and relevant to children's developmental and psychological needs. It wasn't lost on me that someone, probably Joanne Wiens, didn't use the typical 'integration of faith and learning' statement, which seems to make up so many Christian school mission statements.

I was already being won over to this school and its way of being in the world, a particular way that was producing right relationships. But the mission statement sealed the deal. The mission statement must have been a roadmap that guided this little school. I observed teachers almost daily living as if the mission statement were alive. The experiences of students, kids who trusted their teachers, were informed and affirmed by this mission.

But it was also Joanne's other ideas woven throughout and within her dozens of messages that won me over. With Joanne, it was apparent both words and actions spoke loudly. She wrote about Jesus's teachings being incarnated in so many kids and parents—teachers too. She described experiences and lives that she and her teachers had influenced. Now she has taken on the heavy lifting of putting it all together into this little but important book.

This book isn't one more set of ought-tos, should, and have-tos, how to broker abstractions and facts to kids in Bible classes. Personally, I don't think we need another book like that. This book tells the stories of Joanne's experiences at Menno Simons Christian School, the truth of things as they happened. As G.K. Chesterton once wrote, the most important truth is what things are. The stories Joanne tells are 'what are' for all of us who still care about education that would lay claim to the adjective 'Christian.' They are the signposts, reminding us about the kingdom of God Jesus taught us, a way of being in the world that comes through right relationships with God, others, self, and the created and natural order. Her stories remind us that right relationships are produced when we take up and practice Jesus's teachings.

And isn't that the point of it all?

Now read on. Joanne tells her stories of her years at Menno Simons with warmth and love for a little school. And in so doing, she encourages each of us also to look at our own lives to see moments that may appear routine and ordinary, yet at the same time are simply sacred.

—Dr. Bernie Potvin
Author of *Old Ideas, New Practices. When Religion is for Relationships*

INTRODUCTION

I followed a school around for twenty-three years. Literally. Menno Simons Christian School in Calgary, Alberta, was a school without a permanent place to call its own. Frequently we were forced to find a new building and pack up every textbook, soccer ball, and paintbrush to reestablish ourselves.

Our identity was forged without a home. And while the dream of a permanent spot eventually was gloriously realized, the beauty of wandering was this: we had to look to each other for our sense of belonging. We learned who we were through our relationships, our community, and the beautiful spirit of committed teachers and parents who wanted only to raise up our children in the way of the Lord so they would not depart from it—we learned who we really were. In fact, as exhilarating as it was to see the fruition of a dream—a permanent school home—there were times when I was more than a little anxious. I worried that perhaps we'd lose what was even more precious: a sense that God was intimately with us in our learning and living together, even in our wandering. Perhaps especially in our wandering. There had been no other foundation than that of Christ alone.

Journeying each day with children and youth was a holy calling. The glimpses we were given into students' lives showed us not only the potential of who they would become but also shone the spotlight on the intricate value of who they were, the moments we were living with them each day. While our school motto was "An Education for Life," that didn't apply exclusively to the future. It pointed us toward making the present shared moments equally reverent and worthy. Not even children are guaranteed a long future. The stories that made up our daily experiences were collectively the stories of our lives.

One day on my daily rounds visiting classrooms, I stopped at a young second-grader's desk. He was busy drawing an intricate web of squiggles with a black crayon. I placed my finger on his notebook and said, "That's quite a spider you have there." He looked at me horrified and replied, "That's not a spider. That's Jesus on the cross!" There is no recovery from a glaring gaffe such as that, so I meekly slunk away. But I knew again as I had discovered every day of my work with children and young people: they see things clearly and unencumbered. And it awoke within me a deep desire to avert my gaze from the black, erratic, nonsensical squiggles of the world and see instead the presence of something sacred.

I started to look more intentionally for hints of the divine where I had been mistakenly seeing something else. A scene from the 2019 Notre Dame fire tragedy astounded me. Some of the four hundred firefighters who had attended the blaze went back to survey the damage. It was smoky. A huge pile of black rubble smouldered near the front altar. A gaping hole tore through the dome. But, unbelievably, the golden cross at the altar was glowing.

You couldn't miss it.

Everything around those firefighters spoke of damage, destruction, and despair. So much had been lost. But brilliantly, unashamedly, and almost unbelievably, the cross of Jesus not only remained, it also glowed. It was so radiant that an onlooker almost needed to turn away because it was like looking at the holy dwelling place of God. Vivid and strong, the cross is unchangeable no matter what destruction or hell is around it. It can't be destroyed or even ignored.

My living and learning for many years revolved around the hallways of a school. It was a time that amazed and delighted me, even with its moments of rough spots and despair. I kept stories and articles that I had written, little tidbits of life that amused and inspired me. But when

I left that place I had journeyed in for so long, all the stories went into a box in a crawl space in my basement. When I did a massive basement clean-up, the box of stories went into the recycling bin. As I was walking with a now-empty story box to my house, I had to stop. I couldn't do it. I couldn't throw out stories. It seemed to be sacrilegious.

I had to tip the recycle bin over and rescue those scattered words. I started to string them together in patterns that made sense. And I found that what I saw in those stories was a common thread. It was a shaft of sunlight directing me to the cross. At every corner I turned, every classroom I peeked into, in every hallway conversation I remembered, I now saw a glowing cross that refused to leave. Even when I remembered times of struggle, when it felt like standing in a pile of rubble, I now saw the divine presence of Jesus.

My story is about a school. Yours may be a different context, but I'm sure the cathedral of your life has had tremendous beauty, a few renovations, and maybe even a destructive fire. I hope these glimpses into my schoolhouse will show you that ordinary moments and ordinary days are also sacred moments and sacred days. Maybe they'll remind you of similar moments in your journey. Most of all, I want to show you that Jesus is there in every step. And most brilliantly, the golden cross symbolizing his love and sacrifice glows in the depths of your soul even as the wisps of smoke enhance its beauty. If only you turn to see.

Let me open the school door for you. You will hear the persistent ring of the bell, the easy laughter of children, the squeak of a marker across a fresh piece of paper. You will see teachers taking the stairs to their classrooms two at a time, carrying their coffee cups and the strength of their convictions. You will feel that genuine embrace at the door as the day begins, and also at the end of the day as the coach puts his arm around even the clumsiest player to send him out with an encouraging word to play the game that is life.

In the atrium, through the front doors, streams a bright morning sunbeam. Its tender glance touches all who enter, and it illuminates even the darkest corner. It envelopes everything with its warmth, strength, and most of all, grace. You know what it is when you see it. You feel it in every breath. It's not a confusing squiggle. It's Jesus, God incarnate.

CHAPTER 1

REDEEMED

You came near when I called on you; you said, "Do not fear!" You have taken up my cause, O Lord, you have redeemed my life. (Lamentations 3:57–58)

To be fair, their aim was good. Two egg cartons were strewn carelessly on our front steps, but the twenty-four eggs found their mark on our south side windows with impressive accuracy. They chose a good time of year because it was warm enough that the yellowy yolks and milky whites slowly drifted down the windows, covering a lot of territory—then it got cold enough at night that the mess froze quite nicely. It would necessitate more than a little elbow grease to scrape off. With the morning sun on my back, I surveyed the scene before others came and knew which way my day was headed. I wanted to clean up the worst of the mess before cars with kids started rolling up to the entryway. At the very least, I wanted to ensure they weren't crunching over eggshells, but there was no way I could complete the entire task before school startup.

What our impressive egg throwers hadn't thought of was our security camera located a couple of metres from where they stood firing away, recording their every move. It took time for our IT guy to wade through a weekend's worth of footage, but he forwarded the relevant feed to me by the end of the day. Clear as day were three almost teenage boys rifling eggs at our windows. They were former students, which gave me pause. This vandalism wasn't a random act of bored kids; there was some malcontent there, a message was being sent.

I had learned early on that when a principal makes a phone call to a parent, it's not greeted with glee. Parents jump immediately to one of two possibilities: either their kid is hurt or in trouble. It got to be that I used to start phone calls by identifying myself and immediately adding "…and everything's okay." But I didn't relish calling families of former students and informing them of the weekend's transgressions. I expected disbelief and defensiveness—which I received—and a demand to see the footage, which I was happy to oblige. In the end, I met with each boy and a parent. We asked that they contribute from their allowance to cover the time of our tech and our caretaking team. They put in some sweat equity. It was resolved, but it was a hollow ending to our time together.

I once saw a legal television show that asked a central question that gave me pause. The story involved a businessman who, while driving home drunk after work, hit and killed a youth. He was deeply remorseful and prepared to serve whatever jail time was allotted. On bail, while awaiting sentencing, he came across a playground where a knife-wielding, mentally unbalanced individual was threatening young children. The man intervened without thought, risking his life to take down the knife-wielder and rescue the children. The prosecutor now had a moral dilemma. It was in her legal right to ask for a harsh sentence. Yet, the man had also shown courage and honour. She looked at her prosecuting team and asked, "Do we judge a person by their worst day or their best day?"

Good question. For those of us who, by the nature of our position, have to mete out consequences, where does our lens focus? On the person's worst day or their best day? Around their best qualities or their worst? Going one layer deeper, when we rehash harm that has been done to us, especially when it is egregious, can we reach a state of forgiveness faster by dwelling on the qualities of goodness despite the neon flashing of the hurt caused?

I learned a fast lesson on focusing this lens when I transitioned into the principal's role. I had just met with my predecessor, and while we were still chatting in the outer office, a teacher sent an angry student down. This student was a frequent flyer. He'd been at our school for years and was no stranger to the principal's office.

What caught me off-guard was how warmly the student was greeted. There was every reason to be authoritarian, to roll eyes in frustration, and say 'you again?' But there was none of that. My predecessor greeted the student with kindness, asked how he was doing, and asked if he'd do him a favour by waiting in his office for a few minutes while he finished up some things. I noticed immediately that this gentleness and respect instantly lifted the boy's eyes from the floor. Shame was replaced with the sense that, while a hard discussion might be ahead, he was going to get a fair shake. An all-important tone and connection were established so quickly that restoration was an immediate possibility in both their eyes.

Trust is fragile. When our school moved to a new community, we tried hard to establish ourselves as a contributing part of the neighbourhood. But when two of our older students headed off campus looking for mischief, we took many steps backward. The moment was seemingly spontaneous, unprovoked, and generated somewhere without logic or reason in the teenage brain. While walking by a house, they spotted a garden hose along the side. Sneaking up the pathway, they unwound the hose, placed it in a window well, and turned it on full force. Then they carried on their way. We might never have learned about it except that hours later, the same boys were on an education bike trip and coincidentally happened to head down the same street with their group. They must have had a moment of regret because they slowed to the back of the line, stopped their bikes, and went to turn off the hose. Their teacher spotted the movement, started asking questions, and the dominoes began to fall.

That's how I found myself at 4:00 in the afternoon ringing the doorbell at the same house. A visibly upset elderly lady answered the door. It didn't take much of an introduction and the first of many apologies before she allowed me to accompany her to the basement. The damage was extensive and would take months to restore, with a price tag in the thousands. The news would fly through the neighbourhood much faster. While she was initially appreciative to know the cause and that we would certainly help repair the damage, a sleepless night for her changed all that. Communication stopped, and the police were soon at my office door. The damage wasn't confined to the basement; it was flowing into our school's reputation. At the moment, we weren't known by our best day but by our worst day.

Police protocol follows a stringent pathway. They press charges, and then consequences are meted out. It's a faceless process and doesn't allow for restoration between two parties. I pushed for something different from our faith tradition, a chance for restorative justice. I hoped to bring everyone together: our students, their parents, myself, the police, the victim and her advocate. We would sit together so we could see each other, hear stories, seek forgiveness, and work out a mutual solution. The police were reluctant to follow this direction, and, as arbiters of the discussion, their awkwardness was palpable. But we kept at it, and with the financial generosity and sincere support of the families involved, we made amends as best we could and vowed to do better as neighbours. I think it showed that our boys weren't hooligans but good kids who took a misstep. Their gaze could move from their shoelaces up to the faces of the people around them who were prepared to walk with them. Restoration was possible. We started to move out of our worst day through that circle of responsibility and respect.

> I see JESUS as constantly being in the business of MOVING PEOPLE out of their worst day.

I see Jesus as constantly being in the business of moving people out of their worst day. When Zacchaeus climbed a tree to catch a glimpse of Jesus as he passed by, Jesus not only saw and acknowledged him but invited himself over to Zacchaeus's house (Luke 19). The people grumbled that Zacchaeus was a sinner, but Jesus saw the possibility of redemption. Sure enough, Zacchaeus responded to the Master's intervention by giving back to the poor and others he had wronged. And we can look to other scenarios where Jesus pursued an opportunity—the woman at the well, the rich young ruler, even the thief hanging on the cross beside him in his final agonizing moments—Jesus consistently offered love, compassion, and redemption.

We can do the same. It's not easy, but it is possible. It takes a generous heart, a forgiving nature, and a compassionate outlook. It means letting go of grudges and wounds to acknowledge our common humanity. It means approaching situations with an attitude that lifts a person's eyes from the ground to meet yours.

An old Cherokee teaching his grandson about life said:

> A fight is going on inside me... It is a terrible fight, and it is between two wolves. One is evil—he is anger, envy, sorrow, regret, greed, arrogance, self-pity, guilt, resentment, inferiority, lies, false pride, superiority, and ego. The other is good—he is joy, peace, love, hope, serenity, humility, kindness, benevolence, empathy, generosity, truth, compassion, and faith. The same fight is going on inside you—and inside every other person, too.
>
> The grandson thought about it for a minute and then asked his grandfather, "Which wolf will win?"
>
> The old Cherokee simply replied, "The one you feed."[1]

Let's feed the good wolf. Let's walk towards restoration. Let's see people as who they are on their best day. And then, just maybe, we can hope someone will do the same for us. Although wait, that's already happened—we call him Saviour. He calls us Redeemed.

---

[1] "An Old Cherokee," *Quite Frankly*, September 12, 2020. (https://www.quitefrankly. tv/quite-frankly-originals/2020/9/12/)

CHAPTER 2
NOT WINNING THE RACE

Therefore, since we are surrounded by so great a cloud of witnesses, let us also lay aside every weight and the sin that clings so closely, and let us run with perseverance the race that is set before us, looking to Jesus the pioneer and perfecter of our faith, who for the sake of the joy that was set before him endured the cross, disregarding its shame, and has taken his seat at the right hand of the throne of God. (Hebrews 12:1–2)

By some odd quirk, I remember my first year of teaching as clearly as if it were yesterday. Not necessarily the years that followed, mind you, but that first year is crystal clear. On a sleepless night a while back, I could remember every student's first and last name in my first Grade three class. I remembered their foibles and successes, the boy that threw up all over his desk during math, the boy I drove to the hospital with a broken arm, and the way the class giggled when I threw objects at the walls to keep the squeaky resident bats quiet. And I distinctly remember the boys' relay race on a sunny and bright June morning.

There was a considerable rivalry between our small town and our closest neighbours, and at the end of the combined town track-and-field day, each grade had a competing town relay. I was eager for my boys to race because they were fast. We trained at lunchtime for weeks, practicing passing the baton and staying in our lane.

On race day, we were a little edgy and nervous. It was a big deal. We wanted to win. Well, as luck would have it, the first pass wasn't a good one; we fumbled the baton and fell behind. The boys didn't give up though, and slowly started making up the difference. Even so, when our last runner got the baton, we were… well… losing by a fair margin. It was, however, an amazing sight. Our anchor runner was as quick as lightning, and with everyone wildly cheering—okay, me—he steadily gained ground on his opponent. At the last moment, he caught up, and in a feat of Olympic-like calibre, leaned his body over the finish line for the win. We were truly ecstatic. The thrill of victory was exhilarating. I confess that I'm sure I made some boastful comments.

With the passage of time and further life experience, I no longer look at that event the same way. In fact, the news flash from Hebrews 12 is that the race isn't about winning; it is about perseverance. The previous verses in Hebrews 11 give us a long list of faith followers, and I realize it's not a list of winners; it's a list of people who persevered, who carried the torch, not to the finish line but the torch for the gospel. And the gospel of peace says the first shall be last in his kingdom.

If the race isn't about winning, what is it about? So what if you aren't going to be successful? What if you aren't popular? What if you aren't employed? Maybe you aren't going to be healthy. What if God is asking you to be faithful and persevere even though life isn't as expected? What if our saddest moments, our dark nights of the soul, our depression, our loneliness, our hard times are as much a part of the race as the moments of joy? Would we have been told to persevere if everything was going to be alright?

I return to that first race of my teaching career and wonder—did I miss the mark? Out of that team, two boys tragically died young in separate car accidents, and one is now living with cancer. Did I teach them to win or persevere? Did I teach them to have joy in their living, compassion for those around them, a sense of wonder for their world? Or did I tell them that life was about being the best? It is attributed to Ralph Waldo Emerson that, "The purpose of life is not to be happy. It is to be useful, to be honourable, to be compassionate, to have it make some difference that you have lived and lived well."[2] What a paradigm

---

[2] This quote has been attributed to different people and is popularly considered to belong to Ralph Waldo Emerson. Since it can't be determined with certainty, and sources go back some time, it's considered as being in the public domain.

shift in thought—if we were to wish for ourselves and even our children, not happiness, but to live well... no matter what.

I was interested to read that a hundred-kilometre race was initiated in Nepal. Thought to be the most difficult race globally, a trekker would hike it in five days. A strong, long-distance runner could race it in twelve hours. The course has been described as unforgiving along a steep, uneven mountain track. So challenging is the course that a backup team follows along behind the racers, including the possibility of emergency helicopter rescue.

Perhaps this race is more like our life map than we know. We aren't prepared even if we think we are. More often than not, loose stones and steep gullies cause us to slip, fall, and despair that the journey is too hard. But, and what a joyful conjunction that is, *but* there is a backup team. They are called the cloud of witnesses. They are called your church community. They are called your spiritual mentors in the faith. They are the backup team that is led by Jesus Christ. We look to the cross for meaning. It isn't something you merely put your hands on. It isn't something you wear. The cross is something you bear.

I learned more about the gospel of peace later in my career at a girls' basketball game. In a scramble for the ball, our fastest player got the ball and started for the net. In the tangle of limbs reaching for the ball, her closest opponent was tripped and fell. With the way clear for a layup and an easy two points... and in fact with her coach yelling (yes, again me in this position) for her to drive to the basket... our player did the unthinkable. She stopped to see if the opposing player was injured. She stopped and helped her up.

She didn't win the race. But that play has stuck in my mind more than any basketball championship I've been involved in. Because that player knew better than I the true meaning of the race. Her gut instinct was to stop and help. If I could reverse time and have my group of relay racers back, I'd tell them something different. I'd say that the race is about how we run it. It's about running with integrity. It's about stopping our personal pursuit to lend a hand to someone else. It's about compassion for the least of our neighbours, not the most important. It's about speaking out on injustices in our small day-to-day world and in the global community. It's about being the person who doesn't win but perseveres despite the trials. It's about keeping your eyes on Jesus. Because if we truly believe in the gospel of peace, if we take it to heart, if we are peacemakers with all humankind, there can be no other way.

Tie your shoes tight and get ready to run. The race may not be easy. But even then, we can feel God's presence around us, cloaking us in righteousness, truth, and the joy of the Spirit. We are surrounded by a great cloud of witnesses, strengthened by their example, affirmed by their love, and placed gently by God's hand beside them in the story of faith.

CHAPTER 3
THE DOOR CRACKS OPEN

*For I have great joy and encouragement from your love,
because the hearts of the saints have been refreshed through
you....* (Philemon 1:7, CSB)

In the first week of my principalship, I was boxing up a classroom and moving into an office when I found myself surrounded by a group of seven-year-olds. The topic of conversation was my new job.

"So, you're going to be the new principal?" they queried.

"Yes," I said, sensing an opportunity, "what should I do?"

Their response was immediate, "Let kids chew gum and punish bad kids." While I might question their use of words, there was a nugget of truth there. In working with children, there is a balance between grace and accountability. We are in the business of educating and nurturing children. We want to challenge their minds, developing in them a spirit of service, and encourage them to walk the path of their lives with our Saviour. And in all these areas, we hold kids responsible for doing their best, to encourage and affirm them, and giving them the grace they need when they fall short. It all starts at the door that lets in cracks of joy.

I tried to start my early mornings just inside the doors of the school atrium to greet kids and parents, pass out hugs, and get caught up on our community news. Actually, as usual, the kids explained my role best. A young student coming up to the door said to his carpool driver, "That lady—she's always waiting for us." Well, yes, I was. It was a joyful way to start the day.

On sunny days there wasn't a more beautiful spot in the school. The sun rose and poured through those many windows, and to bask in that glory while young people and children trooped through the doors was usually a perfect beginning to the day.

On wet or snowy days, the kids knew I wouldn't let them past without removing their shoes, so standing with my hands free often preceded a handoff while they gave me their treasures to hold while they took off their wet boots and shoes. I gingerly held much-loved, ragged stuffies—show and tell objects destined for the classroom, projects held together with toothpicks and marshmallows, more than one volcano intended for eruption, artwork created by a loving child for their teacher—and even babies! One day a young boy who had been on vacation bounded through the door with a smile on his face. "How was your holiday?" I asked.

"I just *knew* you were going to ask me that!" he replied as he launched into a detailed description. Thank goodness I had asked!

Sometimes the news at the door wasn't good. "How was your weekend?" I asked a mother who was uncharacteristically without children hanging on to her.

"Not good," she rattled off, almost dispassionately, "I had a miscarriage." I quietly drew her to the side, away from the throng, and the words and tears tumbled out.

One eight-year-old girl came in on a Monday morning, looking completely askew. Her backpack was trailing more items than Gretel's crumbs in the forest, and she threw her coat, lunch, and backpack items down at my feet. Plopping herself down to remove her shoes, she started in, "Well, that was a lousy weekend." I didn't say anything, just bent down to the knot in her laces and started to untangle it. Her next words were the game changers and as tangled as her laces. "My parents are getting divorced." For what seemed like the millionth time in my career, I thanked God for this doorway that not only opened doors to the school but gave me an opening to the heart. I now had my game plan for the day. I bundled up that unwieldy backpack and accompanied our girl to her class. I gave the teacher a heads up about what would be influencing this child this day, and then I headed to my office to start the phone calls. It was a life-changing moment for the kids. It was a holy moment for the staff to walk along this divide in their lives. And in the months ahead, every time a little teary face appeared at my door, I cleared everything for a cuddle. Even challenging situations had cracks of joy.

Sometimes the appearance at the door was unexpected. One day a knock came in the form of two Grade three students. It was about 5:00, almost time to pack up and go home, and they were waiting for their older siblings to finish track practice. Giggling and looking very pleased with themselves, they slipped into my office and moved some chairs to face my desk. "We're here to talk about our children," they began, "can you tell us how they are doing?" What could I do but play along? I swivelled away from my computer and launched into an explanation of the recent experiences "their children" had had at school. We seriously discussed (at their initiative) reading and spelling difficulties, as well as positive strides they had been making. We delved into the area of behaviour issues and discussed our common struggle in motivation. Not once did this "parental couple" lose their character or forget who they were. In fact, at one point, one of their "children" wandered in and was immediately admonished for his behaviour. He, too, slipped into character, sat meekly between them on the floor, and the discussion continued. When their "real" parents were suddenly calling their names to head home, they thanked me very politely for my time and hightailed down the hallway. I smiled all the way home. I didn't want to forget for one minute why we were here or who this school was for—the kids. And all of them, with their combined energy, imagination, and good fun, were the greatest gifts. They gave us such joy.

But once, to my shame, I slammed a door. An older student had been sent to me by his teacher, vibrating with anger. I was pressing him about what had happened when he exploded out of his chair. Knocking it over, he lunged at me, yelling. I could only think to escape, and because I had a clear exit to the door, I hurried out and slammed it shut.

As the door shut, a large wooden key I treasured fell off the door and shattered. I was immediately chastened. That key had been a gift when I began my job—with the admonition that being the resident of the principal's office meant I had a figurative key with me at all times—a key to the lives of students, to some of their worst places and some of their best. A key to conversations with parents as I heard information that could be heart-wrenching. I held a key that brought me into the world of teachers, sometimes their classrooms, and often their personal lives. That key was sacred—not to be taken lightly. And there it lay, shattered. I had broken a trust, and I hung my head. I knew that I would never slam another door. But I also knew I could walk back in. I picked up the pieces and walked back into a room where I needed to make amends, a room that wasn't about me but about one so hurting he was out of control. I walked in because it was my job to help, not bail. I walked in because a knock on my door was mine to honour, no matter how difficult.

In the gospel of John, Jesus uses the imagery of a door. He says early in Chapter 10, *"The one who enters by the gate is the shepherd of the sheep. The gatekeeper opens the gate for him, and the sheep hear his voice. He calls his own sheep by name and leads them out"*(John 10:2,3). It was a privilege at our school to have the opportunity to be at the door and offer a hand, showing children the way to the door. Our faith infused all parts of our living and learning at our school, and our teachers regarded most highly those moments where we stood on holy ground. Perhaps this was when we prayed with students over difficult situations; perhaps it happened when we sang together, perhaps it occurred when a student told a teacher they were ready to decide to commit their life to Christ. Jesus enters the door ahead of us. And most remarkably, he knows our name, and he is our Gatekeeper. It is our hope and prayer that when students entered our doors, they also entered into a relationship with the One who stands at the door of life, waiting.

CHAPTER 4
PUZZLE PIECES

*Then Esau looked up and saw the women and children.
"Who are these with you?" he asked. Jacob answered, "They
are the children God has graciously given your servant."*
(Genesis 33:5, NIV)

There was an unusual buzz around our hallway bulletin board. One of our teachers, in an entrepreneurial spirit, had brought 120 three-dimensional posters to school, which she decided to sell for $2.00 apiece and contribute the funds to the school. Arranged on the bulletin board were the different samples one could buy. A 3-D poster (for the unenlightened) on one level is a picture of repeated patterns. As you focus on the picture, another picture emerges, completely unconnected with the repeated patterns, and apparently, the picture jumps out at you in 3-D.

I'm not a believer. I can't see the 3-D pictures, although I've had lots of advice. A group of Grade nine students took it upon themselves as their mission to help me. Their suggestions ranged from, "Stand really close, focus, and then slowly move back until the picture appears," or, "Cross your eyes and let it come at you." One Grade nine tutor was in a fit of giggles as she tried to get me to cross my eyes. One of our teachers unhelpfully added that crossing her eyes was a skill she learned while fixing her eyes on the pattern in the tablecloth during family devotions! For some reason, it's a skill I've never learned. It was frustrating to hear cries of, "Oh, do you see the stegosaurus?" around me and not be able to see a thing. I had company in my misery. A fellow teacher had threatened to tear all the posters down (in a peace-loving kind of way, of course) because if he couldn't see the picture, why should anyone else? And when one of our Grade five students finally caught me stealing yet another unrewarded gaze during class time and said, "Don't worry, Ms. Wiens, I can't see it either," I decided to give up the challenge.

These weren't the only puzzles in school that baffled me. Sometimes a principal's job is part detective. A scenario may slowly unfold, but like a sleight-of-hand, you don't see it until it's full-blown. Take the case of the missing locks. Our Junior High students decided that they could be more efficient if they didn't lock their lockers completely between classes. They left the locks hanging partially open, requiring just a pull or one digit away from opening. And then the locks started disappearing. Not all at once, maybe one a day, maybe a couple in an afternoon. Nothing was taken from the lockers, just the locks.

Of course, we had the students return to fully locking their locks, but we were missing at least a dozen locks. We did the obvious searches of lockers and classroom shelves with no luck. It was a bit of a surprise then when the mother of a Grade two boy showed up in my office some days later. She had a bag with her that she'd found stuffed in a closet at home, and there were our locks. This wasn't a Junior High culprit after all! She handed me the bag and said she would leave the inquisition to me. And so into my office shuffled a young boy, head down, taking his seat with swinging legs. The sun was dancing through the slits in the blinds lightly landing on our boy. I showed him the bag, and he visibly paled. He softly answered my questions about how and what had happened, but the big question I had was, "Why?" His answer floored me, and I can hear his confession to this day. With legs still swinging, he whispered, "I like to hear them tick." It was perhaps the most innocent response I ever heard in that office. I hid my smile, but I wanted to jump up and say, "That is a brilliant answer!" I could just imagine this kid in his dark closet, surrounded by locks, listening for a click that would give him a clue to how to open it. This wasn't subterfuge, no prank to get at kids, no mean-spirited attack. This was a curious—and sneaky—little boy who wanted to hear a lock tick and figure out how it worked. I like to think of that incident as innocence personified.

I liked those puzzles. More complex and more rewarding were the puzzles of the students themselves. What was it about a particular Kindergarten boy that caused him to vehemently refuse to wear a coat on the most blustery of days? Why, suddenly, did a Grade one boy refuse to be more than a metre from his teacher for weeks on end? How did one get a shy new student to stop following teachers around at recess and engage with a peer? What to do with the interminable energy of twin boys, who shimmied up every pole in sight, chased rabbits down back alleys, crashing into garbage bins in their pursuit, and climbed down deep drain holes in the playground cement and became happily stuck below ground? Some puzzles were just ones to shake your head at. Others were explored to see if a clearer picture would emerge.

But some puzzles were unsolvable. Gus had every quality needed to succeed—smarts, charm, and dimples that bracketed his smile. He arrived at our school after becoming entangled in a rough peer group in his previous school where things were spiralling out of control. A change of environment was potentially a change of direction, and we agreed to do what we could. We stumbled along with Gus for a couple of years, but our efforts to help redirect him were fruitless without his cooperation.

It became almost impossible to get Gus to come into the school building, and even if he arrived, he was a runner. I'd hear a door burst open and leap from my desk to the sidewalk just to see his flapping shirt and low-slung jeans racing down the sidewalk, away from help, away from pleas to stay, towards destruction. He missed so many days of school that he was mandated to go to the government Attendance Board, which acts similarly to a court of law. And while Gus was "ordered" to come to school, it was the beginning of the end of our capacity to help him. He transferred to a larger Junior High that I knew would hold even more opportunities for misdemeanour. On his first day in his new school, he was carrying a knife in his pocket, and when he pulled it out, he was expelled.

I lost track of Gus for a while, but when he resurfaced, it was in the most heartbreaking of ways. The next pictures I saw of Gus were chilling. He had a new moniker—notorious gangster and murderer. In the midst of a gang war, Gus arrived at a restaurant in our city, pulled out a forty-five calibre handgun, and in a hail of bullets murdered three people, wounding another. He received a life sentence with no chance of parole for twenty-five years.

This was a puzzle we hadn't come close to solving. How can it be that a child grows up in a Christian home, is taught the scriptures, has the advantage of Christian teachers and parents who care for his heart, soul and mind, can point a gun at another person and shoot them seven times and then turn and shoot more people? I don't have the answer to that, but I know that we show all our kids the repeated patterns as seen in a 3-D poster. Here is God's love. Here is the Good Shepherd. Here is the One who calls you Beloved. But does the real picture pop out? Does the life of Jesus come alive in their hearts?

I can regale you with stories of other students, those who came from more difficult life scenarios yet so embraced what they were taught that they turned their lives around and today influence many people across the globe for God's kingdom. The picture popped out for them, and they never averted their gaze. The seeds planted and watered bore fruit. In the parable of the sower, Jesus talked about how the seed may not take hold. In fact, with rocky soil, or crippling thorns, or pesky birds snatching the seed, there seem to be more threats than easy growth. So, too, with our children. We teach, admonish, and pray for their salvation until we have calluses on our knees. But we may not see that seed take root.

> The GREAT mystery of our GOD is his infinite capacity for LOVE and his tender call to return to HIM.

But here's what I also know. The gaze of Jesus, our Lord and Saviour, never leaves even the most hardened criminal. The great mystery of our God is his infinite capacity for love and his tender call to return to him. The familiar words from F.M. Lehman's hymn, *The Love of God,* talk about how wide and deep God's love is, especially for those who struggle most:

The love of God, is greater far
Than tongue or pen can ever tell;
It goes beyond the highest star,
And reaches to the lowest hell.[3]

When the children and young people in our lives find themselves in difficulty, our continued push is one of faithfulness, loving each child in our care for as long as we have them, reflecting the light of a great and mighty God. This is our calling. Because these are the children God has given to us, his servants, and they too shall be called redeemed.

---

[3] F.M. Lehman, "The Love of God," 1917 (Public Domain).

CHAPTER 5
A TALE OF TWO FIRES

And I tell you that you are Peter, and on this rock I will build my church, and the gates of Hades will not overcome it. (Matthew 16:18, NIV)

I skittered into the lunchtime classroom, alerted by the noise, and their anger was sizzling like a live wire between them. The boys separated as I entered, but their fists were still taut. It wouldn't have taken much for them to explode at each other again. Given that they were bigger and stronger, my options were limited, so I did the only thing I could think of. I turned and headed back out the door and threw a backhanded comment of "Follow me" at them and, without looking back, prayed all the way to my office that they actually would. One boy was unrepentant, unable to look past the hurt and scorn clouding his eyes. But in the second boy, I caught a glimmer of something intangible. Lifting his head from his swelling hands, he looked straight at me and said, "I am trying to remember that in this school, I don't need to act like that." I didn't need to say anything more. He was figuring out a life lesson. Just from absorbing the atmosphere and example of those around him, and because of his receptive heart, he was learning a new way. The spark now ignited had the chance to flare if we could nurture it.

Sometimes life lessons come like the crackle of a fire. What's captivating and mesmerizing about a campfire is the sudden explosion and pop that sends a scattering of sparks in many directions. Some sparks shoot all the way outside the circle of stones, some go straight up into the night sky, and some just fizzle out. But when the spark catches and flares and then settles into constant, glowing embers, there is a quality that is alive and enduring.

Twice in the New Testament, Peter sees the sparks fly around the fire and finds himself staring into the coals—staring into two of the most pivotal moments of his life. Now, Peter's walk with Jesus isn't without blunders. No one questions his enthusiasm or zeal. He loves Jesus and wants to follow him. More than any other disciple, we have evidence of Jesus personally instructing Peter. But in many ways, Peter's early attempts follow the pattern of the familiar good news/bad news stories. The good news is that when Jesus walked on water through a storm, Peter had amazing courage and put his feet out of the boat and walked towards Jesus on the water. The bad news is that he lost faith rather quickly and began to sink.

The good news is that Peter could say enthusiastically that Jesus is the Christ. The bad news is that as soon as he said it, Jesus predicted, "Yet you will deny me three times."

The good news is that Jesus told Peter that he was the rock on which he would build his church. The bad news is that shortly afterwards, Jesus said to Peter, "Get behind me, Satan, you are a hindrance to me."

The good news is that Peter went with Jesus into the garden of Gethsemane to stay with him in his final hours. The bad news is that he fell asleep.

The good news is that Peter was close to Jesus when Judas betrayed him. The bad news was that to show his loyalty, he cut off the soldier's ear, clearly misunderstanding Christ's teachings.

This brings us to our first fire at the foot of the cross. I imagine Peter's mind is reeling. So much had happened: the final supper, the shocking betrayal by a fellow disciple, and now Jesus is under guard. With the disciples scattered, Peter looked for a little comfort around the fire while pondering his next move. The fire crackled as a maid recognized him. A spark shot up as another person placed Peter in Jesus's group. A log fell in a flurry of light as a man insisted he recognized Peter's accent as Galilean. Each time, Peter, the disciple who first recognized Jesus as the Messiah, the disciple who wanted Jesus to wash not just his feet, but his whole head and hands as well—this disciple denied he even knew Jesus. And when the cock crowed, I wonder what passed between the master and the disciple in that look. We know only that the disciple left that fire and wept bitterly.

I'm not being hard on Peter. Unfortunately for him, his failure is recorded in the Bible for us to read. If it were me, if the spotlight shone on my reactions and responses, I wouldn't come out any cleaner. Each of us, despite our love for Jesus and our best intentions, falls short. We're staring at the fire when others approach us about our allegiances, and we get it wrong. This is the fire of denial. In our shame, we go into the dark cold, and we weep bitterly.

The second fire is on a beach after the resurrection. Peter went back to what he knew best, and we find him fishing with the others, but the night was fruitless, and they didn't catch anything. The day was breaking, and the sun was rising. A somewhat familiar man on the beach offered fishing advice. Jumping into the water, Peter met his teacher again at another fire, this time when Jesus was going to cook breakfast. Was it awkward? Did Peter hang his head and apologize? We know that in a brilliant move of forgiveness and establishing a launching place for what will come next, Jesus asked Peter three times to declare his love. This was a poignant act of redemption for Peter—as if the three denials at the first fire were stamped out by three affirmations of love at the second. Jesus finds a way to forgive, heal, and send Peter out to "tend the sheep." This is the fire of redemption.

What happened after the fire of redemption? The concluding scenes are riveting. Peter became the rock upon which the church is built. He became a leader among the disciples. He was a brilliant orator. He became a healer. He was imprisoned and brought before the rulers and elders, where he confidently defended Christ.

What if Peter stayed stuck at the fire of denial? What if he had thought of all the times he didn't measure up, the areas he lacked, the times he bungled what he was supposed to do? Or let's cast our net a bit further. What if Moses had refused to lead the people because he couldn't speak in front of the crowd? What if Joseph gave up when he was thrown into prison and decided just to languish there? What if Esther lacked the courage to confront the king and just expected someone else to intervene? What would have happened if Ruth stayed among the comfort of her people rather than follow her mother-in-law Naomi to a strange land? And let's cast our net out one more time: What if you and I use our excuses to stay stuck? What if we spend our lives at the fire of denial? How will God's kingdom be built? A lump of coal can become a diamond. It is through God's refining fire that we become the people he intended us to be.

We serve the KINGDOM when we catch a glimpse of a SPARK in those around us and fan it to become an ember for God's GLORY.

We serve the kingdom when we catch a glimpse of a spark in those around us and fan it to become an ember for God's glory.

Davis spent a good chunk of his school years in our school. Honestly, it was unremarkable. He hung around the edges of a group; he tossed a shy smile at his classmates and teachers. But relatively unknown to his teachers, he was quietly absorbing, thinking, and learning. We were oblivious, but the Spirit of God was not. A growing glow of embers was getting ready to flare. When Davis the boy became a man, he was a Peter. He became a leader for societal change and travelled the world, sharing his message and provoking large-scale growth. He used his platform to confidently speak about the love of God and the need to turn to him. He took enormous risks. He challenged injustice. Thousands of miles away, I observed this and shook my head. I wouldn't have picked this kid for that task or seen it coming.

When I coincidentally ran into him on leave, we shared a laugh recalling that long ago lunch time ruckus. I told him how proud I was of him. I also told him that the power of the gospel in his life thrilled my heart. In comments completely unexpected, he said, "I am convicted to do much of what I do today because of what I learned at our school." Our school. Our boy. Our Saviour.

Left alone after our encounter on a sunny sidewalk, I hung my head and said, "Lord, forgive my unbelief. How truly great you are."

Jesus was a teacher for life. Our Lord and Saviour, in his most taxing time, gave us a supreme example of mentoring through forgiveness and redemption with his disciple Peter. With the love of Christ supporting and enveloping us, we can move away from the place of brokenness. Even if we have turned away from his soulful gaze at the fire of the cross, there is another fire flickering. It beckons beyond our sightline if we will only move towards it. We are also closely entwined with those entrusted to us to nurture, counsel, and pray with them when they are at their fires of denial. We are called to assure them that Jesus waits with great love for them at the fire of redemption—if they will catch his image and inch forward, moving towards the fire he's tending, waiting for them.

Our greatest gift to our children is to help place them in the story of faith. Their story is a pivotal chapter in the book of history. It begins with the creation of the world and meanders through Adam and Eve, Abraham and Isaac, to Noah, Jacob, and Joseph. It totters on through Esther, Rahab, and Ruth, to David, Solomon, Jeremiah, and Isaiah. Our children and young people need to place themselves in the same story as a humble carpenter called Joseph and a young teenage girl named Mary, who were so filled with the Spirit that they heard and accepted the message from an angel—they would raise a baby who would be the Messiah. And wonder of wonders, within that baby of unpretentious birth was the spark of the fire of redemption.

This brings us back to a discerning boy in my office with his head in his bruised hands after a fight. The embers tentatively catching light in his soul became ablaze as he became a mighty warrior for God, a man with his own chapter of faithfulness in the book of life.

CHAPTER 6

THE WATERS ARE STIRRED

For an angel went down at a certain time into the pool and stirred up the water; then whoever stepped in first, after the stirring of the water, was made well of whatever disease he had. (John 5:4, NKJV)

Okay, here's my confession right off the start. The Grade ones and I were reading through a book about the miracles of Jesus. We were on the dramatic story from John 5 where Jesus heals the crippled man on the Sabbath at the Pool of Bethesda. It begins with the riveting opening of an angel stirring up the water and many invalids waiting to be the first to enter. Whoever was first would be healed. Our book had a great picture of the angel tipping a wing into the water, creating ripples. When we got to that part and observed the picture, I looked at the Grade ones—and in a huge faux pax for a Christian Education teacher, I said—"Well, could that happen?" To which they chorused, *"No!"* and we went on to read about Jesus healing the crippled man—which, of course, we all believed. This didn't sit well with me, and I started having a conversation with myself while continuing the lesson. How could it be that with one random, ill-thought question, I was able to create doubt in the minds of these young children so easily? Why was I questioning the stirring of the waters? In fact, core to my belief is that in our gathered community, the Spirit of the Lord is stirring and awakening our hearts and minds each day. So, the next day, same chapter in hand, I started over and talked about anticipating the work of Jesus in our lives, the stirring of the water.

This is what the story is about: Jesus had gone to Jerusalem for one of the Jewish festivals. The festival isn't specified, but it's thought to have been the celebration of the Passover—the Jewish exodus from Egypt. By the Sheep Gate was the Pool of Bethesda. On the one hand, the picture is appealing—a serene pool with a wall of five arched porches behind it. But what you need to visualize is a crowd of the downtrodden and infirm, those rejected and ignored—waiting. Those lying in the porches—a multitude—are blind, paralyzed, and excluded. We've heard the word *multitude* before: there were a multitude of angels appearing to the shepherds to announce the birth of Jesus. Jesus spoke to the multitudes. So the number of infirm at the pool isn't a small group, and suddenly those porticos were crowded, teeming with the needy who were waiting.

In that group is our main character, a man crippled for the last thirty-eight years. He's waiting at that pool because it was known to be stirred by an angel, giving it healing powers. Jesus comes to him at the Sheep Gate by the porch. Jesus knew the man had been ill a long time and asked if he wanted to be well. The man replied that he had no one to help him get into the water, and no matter how hard he tried, someone else always got there first. Jesus instantly healed him, instructing him to take his mat and walk.

As I studied this passage more, I realized that it isn't without controversy. In fact, my friend, a professor of Church History and a Bible scholar, says it is one of the passages that troubles him the most. Part of the problem is that some scholars consider the reference to the angel stirring the waters to be a legend. It may not have been in early manuscripts. The RSV and the NRSV don't include it—they skip right from verse three to verse five without mentioning the angel's wing tipping into the pool.

While I'm not a biblical scholar and don't want to stake my claim on verse four, what I settled my mind on is that the stage had already been set for Jesus's intervention. Others had already been healed, and there was a sense of anticipation that healing would occur again, enough so that a man is willing to wait "a long time" for it to happen. And yet, Jesus still intervened. He knew the intimate details of the man's life. He knew of his waiting and struggles. What Jesus questioned was the man's will. Did the man want to get better? There are no questions about the man's holiness or the state of his heart. The significant factor is that, without fanfare, Jesus would heal him—because he wants to be made well.

God sets the stage—Jesus intervenes. Really, this is no different than our lives today—if we had the courage to look, each of us would find ourselves at one point or another unable to move, unable to be healed, unable to deal with the hand we have been dealt. If we started from the premise that among us, around us, and in us, it's the work of the Holy Spirit who will intervene on our behalf... would we approach life differently? This heightened awareness provides a deeper understanding, perceiving God lovingly moving in our midst. It is a realization that God has set the stage of events in our lives, a stage precipitated by God, provoked by God, and he comes to us in the tangible form of Jesus.

One summer, as I was preparing for the new school year, I was in frequent email correspondence with a former school family, Don and Karen, who were missionaries in Mozambique. They were working in an orphanage, and the situation became explosive. One of the nationals employed there had beaten a child and was fired by the other missionary couple in the compound. The nationals staged a protest, which turned into a riot. They locked the compound. They denied the missionaries access to the children in the orphanage, including locking thirty babies in the Baby House without an adult. They turned against the missionary family who fired the worker—locking the wife into a storage container. Finally, with the help of police, they were driven safely away, never to return.

Don and Karen kept their children behind locked doors. If further revenge was going to happen, they and their children were in danger. They were greatly restricted in movement and had to watch their children closely while still trying to reach the babies and other children in their care. After their fellow missionaries were driven out of the compound and the situation calmed down, Don and Karen broached the topic of returning to Canada. One night, Don went outside and walked for a long time, speaking to God. "God, if we are to return, we'll need a house." Five hours later, the renters in their Calgary home emailed them and asked for an early exit from their rental contract, effective September 1ˢᵗ. Answer number one.

When I arrived at work one morning, there was an email from Karen asking that, should they return, would I have room for their children at our school, or could I at least put them on the waitlist? Given that their children's placement was in our full early grades, she recognized that the chances were slim. Shall we say by chance, or shall we say by God's design, a family had just suddenly withdrawn, and I had spaces available in the grades she needed. The early morning sun was just peaking over the horizon as I emailed Karen back and said, "Of course, we have room for you." Her next email was one of those holy moments—it sent a shiver up my spine. Karen told me that while I was responding to her email, she and Don were half a world away, walking back from a meeting where they had resigned their positions. It had been a very difficult meeting. People were crying and begging them to stay. Karen and Don were distraught, especially as they had recently committed to staying in Mozambique, sensing this was God's call. As they walked towards their home, they prayed that God would give them a sign to confirm their decision. They walked into their house and went to the computer. There was my email indicating there was room for their children at our school. Answer number two.

It wasn't really my email—it was God's email, another sign. On the first day of school that fall, it was a young Grade three boy who had made the journey all the way from Mozambique to come to school, who offered a prayer of blessing on the school year to the gathered assembly. I bowed my head, absorbing his words, absorbing that he and his siblings were with us because God had sent them to us. I couldn't quite fathom it. But I knew, without a shadow of a doubt, that a mighty God had stirred the waters in the lives of this family.

I believe the stirring of waters also occurs in our own lives. We come to God as broken people—with foibles, with sin, with hurt, with insecurities. We stumble along the path where God's light shines, not always catching the beam we should be walking in. And yet, and yet—despite all of this—our God, who is infinite, the creator of all, cares for each of us and keeps working with us, stirring the waters of our lives, or intervening directly.

When God stirs in the moments of our day, we find it in us to be compassionate to the least among us, those languishing by the pool. When God troubles the waters in our lives, we find new reservoirs of strength—not only for the spectacular but also for carrying on with the mundane. Where there are also rough places, places of difficulty, or pain, of broken relationships, we need to pray that God will intervene, that he will not only stir the waters but walk among us directly—so that restoration, healing, peace and grace will come to us and to those we live and work with. And then, like the man who lay by the pool, we need to wait with the expectation and the anticipation that God will move and stand among us.

CHAPTER 7
CHASING WITH A TENDER HEART

...and be kind to one another, tenderhearted, forgiving one another, as God in Christ has forgiven you. Therefore be imitators of God, as beloved children, and live in love, as Christ loved us and gave himself up for us, a fragrant offering and sacrifice to God. (Ephesians 4:32–5:2)

On the first day of school, as a symbol of our intent to be peacemakers in our world, we unveiled the doves of peace in our beautiful new building. They became our resident symbols of peacemaking. The idea of the doves came—as many good ideas do—sitting on the deck of my friends Bob and Sheila's cabin. We were thinking of what great things we could do on the first day in our new building during Opening Ceremonies. We'd already decided on cake and ice cream (the ice cream having become a first-day tradition), speakers, singing, greeters at the door—but we wanted something extra special. For a long time we threw around the idea of releasing balloons. Or homing pigeons, or butterflies. But it was Sheila who came up with the idea of owning a permanent symbol of our very own doves. I admit to not jumping on that bandwagon, but the deal was clinched when I was told I would *never* have anything to do with them.

In the intervening years, Sheila was good to her word. We named our doves after our school—Milky Menno and Silky Simon, although, with further anatomical inspection, Simon became Simone. With the help of various students, Sheila looked after—and loved—our doves. And they were a hit. Young children were drawn to the cage as they entered, and many of our students looked in on them regularly. When Milky and

Simone escaped their cage one day, two teachers spent their after-school hours patiently moving a ladder around our atrium trying to rescue them.

Later, Sheila pulled our science teacher over to the cage in despair, thinking the Junior Highs were playing a trick on her by putting a rubber chicken in the cage. The science teacher gently informed her that Sheila was a grandmother—the rubber chicken was a baby dove. We called him Christian, and we had one more to look after.

But then Milky Menno became sick. He was literally henpecked. His neck and head had been battered by Silky Simone (not a good peacemaking example anymore!), and he looked—well—under the weather. One of our young girls refused to go out for recess because she didn't want Menno to "die alone." Well, that was the final straw, and before I knew it Menno was isolated and in intensive care *in my office*. How did that happen? During visiting hours, he had a steady stream of concerned visitors—and wait for it, it gets even worse—in this state of heightened anxiety, I even agreed to pay for a visit to the Doctor of Birds' office. I know that my farm family is shaking their head. We saw animals differently. Except for maybe my youngest cousin, who once fled the butchering scene at her farmyard, tears flying, doors slamming, and the words, "I have feelings for those chickens, you know!" echoing to the bewildered farmer holding the axe. Oh well. Swing.

But we weren't on the farm, so Menno got excellent treatment from the attentive Doctor of Birds, including antibiotics and a new organic diet. And after Menno made it through that crisis, he returned temporarily to my office for a further period of isolation from Simone. I didn't even blink an eye. I just cleared off his place for him. I didn't say a word when Sheila handed me the dove every day to hold him still while she tipped the antibiotics into his beak. I may have even gently cooed at him, getting caught up in the moment. I knew we could get a new dove for less cost, but it seemed that we needed to keep in mind the heartstrings of all the little (and big) dove-watchers and be faithful to the symbolism of our doves of uncertain peace. "God sees the little sparrow fall, it meets his tender view. If God so loves the little birds, I know he loves me too."[4]

---

[4] Maria Straub, "God Sees the Little Sparrow Fall," Public Domain.

Watching young, anxious eyes hovering around a sick dove reminds me of the tender heart of Jesus. Yes, I know he turned over the money changers' tables, cast out demons, and rebuked his closest disciple. I know he rose to the challenge of defying Satan after wandering the desert for forty days. He surpassed the Pharisees in knowledge so that they couldn't corner him. But he also held children on his knee and felt the infinitesimal touch of a bleeding woman, and with a look of compassion, Jesus set a burdened adulteress free. He had, as our childhood song suggests, a tender view. It was that tender view that showed distress when even his most faithful disciples couldn't stay awake beside him at the Garden of Gethsemane. This tender view had him cry out to God to take this cup away from him. And ultimately, it was his tender view on all of us abject sinners that took our sins with him to the horror and the beauty of the cross.

When I moved from my teaching position into the principal's office, the most frequent advice I received was, "You're going to have to develop a tougher skin." I understood the intent behind that admonition and may have even wished it to be so, but it wasn't going to happen. All my life, I had thin skin, which filtered others' feelings straight into my soul. In upper elementary, I remember which girl first wore a bra. That news exploded amongst the girls. It was a curiosity, and a startling hint that growing up was at the cusp for us all. I still remember the thick, blond, single braid down the back of that girl. But even more, I remember her brown eyes and the look of sorrow and hurt as every one of us found a reason to clap her on the back to confirm that, yes, that article of clothing was there. And by lunchtime, that same article of clothing was shoved into a crinkly brown bag in her desk. I know because we scoured it out by sneaking back into school when we should have been out at recess. Opening that bag was like discovering a log of shame in my eye that I could stoop to such hurt.

I moved away from that relatively innocent elementary school to a larger, brasher school in Junior High. It only took one day for me to realize that the red lunch kit with the bunny that my mother had lovingly hand-painted in first grade no longer had any place in my life.

I discarded it and the innocence of childhood overnight, and the next morning I carried my lunch in a brown paper bag like everyone else.

It was then that I met the Queen Bee. She had invaded my world enough that I had asked my mom in bewilderment what I should do if someone didn't like me. A lunchtime incident flared in me a burning glow for injustice done to the least of these. The lunchroom was crowded, noisy, and was patrolled haphazardly by teachers. On that day, I was sitting somewhere on the far outskirts of the Queen Bee's harem. A teacher came by our group and told Queen Bee to pick two people to clean up the residue left from the scatter of remaining lunches after people exited. I knew what was coming. It was in her sneer as she surveyed us, carefully making up her mind who to bestow this unwanted task upon. Inevitably, her gaze lingered on another lackey and me, and so with head down, I got up and picked up everyone's scraps. And while that was one of her daggers whose pierce I keenly felt, my sense of injustice flared at the teacher. His entire methodology was circumspect, but in particular, of all the students he could have picked to give some leadership responsibility to, he had chosen to enhance the power of one who already wielded it badly and hurtfully. Where was his radar? Certainly not on the tenderhearted. I already had an inkling where my future occupation would take me, and I vowed then and there not to enhance the power of the Queen Bee and to look out instead for the tenderhearted.

This brings me back to being a principal with that same thin skin. I had a choice: try to toughen my resolve or see the world through a tender view. I was in the hallway on the first day of school with a young girl plastered against me with arms around my waist. We had sent Mom out the door to facilitate the transition, but I doubted that move now. In my own first week of school as a child, I got kicked out of class and sent to stand in the hallway corner. I wasn't talking out of turn or fooling around. I was sitting in my seat sobbing because my farm seven miles down the road, where the prairie grass bent in the wind, was beckoning me. School was not. Standing in that hallway with tears leaking out of my eyes was the loneliest experience of my young life. And now another little girl's sobs, so wrenching, were undoing me. Going through that classroom door would be positive, warm, and fun for her. She was going to spend the next 189 days skipping through that door. She just couldn't take that first step. I felt her and there was no way I was letting this girl stand in that hallway in her misery all alone.

My office next to the doves' cage was right beside the front doors. I loved it. I could see people coming in, and they would often duck their heads in to see if I had a minute, which I quickly learned meant did I have half an hour. I definitely did. I described my job to a friend that I felt like an "absorber." My role by name alone gave me the honoured position of listening to life's heartbreaking and crucial stories: a parent's anguished concern over their child, a teacher's distress over a miscarriage, a board member's difficult health diagnosis. And yes, inevitably, I also heard someone's sharp barb of anger and frustration over where we had gone wrong as we journeyed together. I absorbed them all, hoping that I took away a little of the person's burden. It was exhausting and exhilarating at the same time. I knew of no other way to go through life.

I once found a torn corner of paper, flung haphazardly onto my desk, with a quickly scribbled note in pencil. Its simplicity was also its profundity: "I'm glad you're my principal because you chase me." That note went into my envelope of Letters Worth Keeping. While I knew it referred to a fun recess, it was a better philosophy of education than any staid university textbook could offer. *I see you over there, and I'm going to chase you.* Across the sundrenched playground, to the fence, around the outdoor basketball court. I see you, and I'm going to chase you when you struggle with a math problem, when you ask me a question whose answer is longer than the time I thought I had, when you sit in my office with your head hung after a bad decision. I see you, and I'm going to chase you till that moment, graduation cap in hand, you exit our doors and my prayers trail after you. My skin may be thin, but my heart is wide, deep, and full. I see you, and I'm going to chase you because it's what God does for each of us. To every corner of the earth. To every pit of hell. To every mountain top. He chases us with a focused pursuit and a tender heart. Go and do likewise. The doves of peace are circling above you as you go.

CHAPTER 8
TAKE A STEP FORWARD

Our steps are made firm by the Lord, when he delights in our way; though we stumble, we shall not fall headlong, for the Lord holds us by the hand. (Psalm 37:23–24)

The school year was in its final, harried month. A Kindergarten boy wandered into my office at lunch. He came right beside where I was working on my computer and started to draw in the dust on my heat register. "So," he began, "I forgot my money for the school store."

"Well," I replied, "I guess you can't buy anything this time round." He didn't seem too happy with that answer and continued drawing his dust picture. There was a little silence while I worked and he drew. "So," he said again, "do you think you could lend me some?" I smiled at his initiative and pulled out some loonies. He was off like a shot, having achieved his purpose.

Ten months earlier, there wasn't a chance this boy would have pulled this off. School routine was new, we were all strangers, and he was figuring it out. And yet, in his little five-year-old brain, he did. Here was a safe place where it was okay to wander into any room. Here were new friends. Every day held things to learn and discover. And in his comfort, he figured out a way to make a lunchtime purchase even though he wasn't prepared. He stepped forward because he was learning and adapting as he moved through the corridors of life.

When did we forget to do the same as adults? Where did we lose the courage to take stalk of our surroundings, see the goal ahead of us, and plunge forward however gently and timidly with a small step? There are small moments on life's journey when we should reach out to connect to someone, yet we don't make the phone call. There are big moments when life has beaten us down, and we can't get past the hurt, the betrayal, the diagnosis. Some people stay there for years. But the only way out is to take a small step forward. And then another.

Clarice was part of our school community before she reached Kindergarten. As the youngest in her family, she had time to observe school life from the sidelines. While her older siblings could barely contain their energy and exuberance of life, Clarice quietly observed and avoided talking to us. We tried; she just looked at us with those soulful eyes. I considered it a success when I enticed her with library books into my Grade one classroom. She sat by herself in the story corner and paged through the books. When she was done, she wordlessly slipped away.

So it was a bit of a shock when the Great Bathing Suit Caper, a story of considerable creativity and deliberate subversive steps, revolved around Clarice. Clarice was now in Grade three, and swimming lessons were mandatory: five days in the pool learning the basics of water safety and swimming. But Clarice didn't want to go. At all. And for each day of lessons, she carefully planned how to get out of swimming.

Day one: Clarice's teacher called at the end of the day to say that Clarice didn't have her bathing suit at school so she couldn't go into the pool, even though her mom had packed it in her backpack the night before. When asked later that day, Clarice said she didn't know where her bathing suit was. Her parents cajoled her, humoured her, and then got a bit more serious, trying to get her to tell them where it was. She said nothing. That evening, while looking for something in the crawl space, Clarice's mom found the suit sticking out from under a suitcase. She confronted Clarice again. With a serious face, Clarice said that Annabelle, the cat, must have taken it out of the backpack and hid it in the crawl space. It was such a surprising and creative comment that it was hard to be mad.

Day two: another call from the teacher. No bathing suit again. This time with a bit more directness, Clarice's parents again confronted her. She gave up nothing. She cried, saying she didn't know where it was. Clarice's parents pushed. Still nothing. Later that evening, as her mom was working outside, she noticed part of Clarice's bathing suit sticking out from underneath a woodpile. Annabelle struck again!

Day three: another call from the teacher. No bathing suit or backpack. Clarice left it in the locker. That evening there was more talking, more tears.

Day four: one more call from the teacher. Clarice had the backpack and the bathing suit. But she said she was feeling sick. Too sick to swim. Clarice sat and watched instead.

Day five: success! Holding out until the last day, Clarice went into the pool and got through the swimming lesson.

It will not surprise you to learn that to this day, Clarice hates swimming. But the beauty of this story is the thought process, creativity, and deliberate action she took to find a way to avoid what all the adults were saying she had to do. While her outward appearance was a calm surface, inside a roaring ocean was roiling and turning and planning. Impressive! But the nugget I take from Clarice's story is her persistent courage. Day after day, new obstacles surfaced. Day after day, plans needed to be made. What worked once may not work again. Keep thinking. Keep deliberating a new course of action. Don't give in.

Persistent courage: asking for a loan for the school store, planning how to get out of swim lessons. Perhaps persistent courage is the hard thing. A shuffle sideways, a ducking of the head, a whimper at what lies ahead, is easier—but all that keeps us stuck short of where we want to be—fixing one's eyes forward, with persistent courage, continuing to take step after faltering step, therein lays strength of character.

On a Sunday afternoon, I was strolling through a downtown park towards a festival with two of my colleagues. The weather was fine, the atmosphere celebratory—until directly in front of us, we saw four youth standing by a bike rack, frantically trying to hide a bolt cutter as we approached. They were in the process of stealing a bike, and unknown to them, three teachers from our school were going to make that job a lot more difficult. I admit, to my shame, that I was prepared to move onward. I wasn't persistent or courageous. We were outnumbered, and they were bigger. Was it *my* job to prevent crime? Fortunately, my colleagues were all of the above.

To my chagrin, we moved right beside that bike rack and carried on a cheerful conversation, reasoning that as long as we stood there, they wouldn't try to steal. We stood and talked; they waited. We stood, they glared. Deciding that this standoff could carry on indefinitely, I left the others in search of help. Frankly, I was happy to escape the tension. I alerted a security person who asked us to keep up our vigil until they could mobilize their people. We did, although as the potential bike stealers saw me talking to an official, they cast us a dark (even scary!) look and lumbered off. We knew, however, that by then, the security people had them in their sights. If these fellows moved to a new spot, they would be watched and apprehended.

And so I kept learning, from children and young people, from the fine people I've worked with. There are things in life worth standing up for. Some situations require deliberate planning to escape. There are hard things that require creativity and care to work through. There are rewards within our grasp, but they may not be easy to attain. All of them require a step forward. All of them require persistence. All of them require courage.

My little Kindergarten friend, at the beginning of this chapter, collected his thoughts and his gumption while he drew in the dust. This reminds me of our Lord, who pondered his next move as he drew in the dirt while the Pharisees tried to trick him into condemning the woman caught in adultery (John 8). They reminded him of the dire consequence in the law of Moses, which required stoning. His fingers grew dusty as he drew, the dirt seeping into his fingernails, and finally, he threw a glance in their direction and made a suggestion: *He who was without sin should cast the first stone.* One sentence did it. Ten words hit the mark. When the Pharisees slunk away outsmarted, he drew in the dirt again, then stood up and this time addressed the woman. With compassion, he sent the woman on her way without condemnation. Instead of facing the end of her life, she was on her way with a fresh slate. Perhaps drawing in the dirt helped Jesus buy some time before responding. And maybe he reflected upon his upcoming supreme act—giving up his life would cover our sins like a hand erasing the dusty drawing of our lives. Maybe he knew that by drawing in the dirt, he was allowing space for the Pharisees to take a more dignified step away; space for a condemned woman to take a grateful step forward into her redeemed life. What a significant lesson of leadership to ponder.

Go and do likewise. No matter what debris is scattered around you, no matter what blow has felled you, no matter what sin has entrapped you, no matter the obstacles between you and your goal, there is a way forward. A slant of sunlight rises over the hill, brilliant and warm. Take a step toward it with persistent courage. The Lord holds you by the hand.

CHAPTER 9
A STILL, SMALL VOICE

...and after the earthquake a fire, but the Lord was not in the fire; and after the fire a still small voice. (I Kings 19:12, NKJV)

There are some tasks you're never warned will fall into your job description as a principal. Among these is setting up the gym for Friday chapel. There were chairs to put out, an ever-multiplying line of lost and found clothes to lay out—hopefully, to entice a kid to pick up their shoes or shirt or jacket. Honestly, given the stash, how did they get home with clothes on their bodies?

And then there was the sound system. For a long time, we used a rickety, hand-me-down portable system. One Friday, a Grade nine student wandered into the gym and started to help me set up. Zeke was graciously fixing my mistaken attempt by adjusting knobs and dials. Even the mic stand looked somewhat askew, and without commenting on my lack of technical prowess, which I deserved, he quickly had everything in working order. We tested the sound, turned it off, and started to walk away. One of us made a comment right beside the mic, and to our surprise, the mic was still live and carried our words across the empty gym. Startled, we looked at each other and glanced back at the controls to ensure that the mic was off. It was. "How did that happen?" I asked. "Do you think it was God?"

Zeke shot me a wry look, and in the wisdom of a young person speaking to an adult, he replied, "If only it was that easy!"

"If only it was that easy…." Copy that. How often that echoes my thoughts in trying to hear God's voice. A voice over the loudspeaker guiding, directing, giving answers to my questions would be less complicated. I wouldn't have to agonize, ponder, and struggle on my own. But maybe that's the point. Zeke suggested that our world and lives are too cluttered, and because of that, it's hard for God to get through. "I like to be hiking on my own," he said, "then I feel closer to God."

I think Zeke was capturing the thoughts of Elijah. Elijah had just had a dramatic encounter in his showdown with the 450 prophets of Baal. When the bull Elijah had prepared was consumed in fire, and the bull of the 450 prophets remained, it was a clear and dramatic sign of God's power. It was a loudspeaker moment. Yet the power of that moment was short-lived, and with Jezebel threatening him, Elijah fled to the wilderness to Horeb, God's mountain. He went where life was uncluttered, where he was alone. Where he could hear the voice of God. Would it be a loudspeaker moment? What follows on that Mount is one of my favourite sections of scripture:

> He said, "Go out and stand on the mountain before the Lord, for the Lord is about to pass by." Now there was a great wind, so strong that it was splitting mountains and breaking rocks in pieces before the Lord, but the Lord was not in the wind; and after the wind an earthquake, but the Lord was not in the earthquake; and after the earthquake a fire, but the Lord was not in the fire; and after the fire a sound of sheer silence. When Elijah heard it, he wrapped his face in his mantle and went out and stood at the entrance of the cave. Then there came a voice to him...
> (1 Kings 19:11–13)

I count on that still, small voice. It is the prod in the heart. It is the way ideas suddenly coalesce into a common theme to move something forward. It is the peace that gently whispers after agonizing over options. It is the sense that while all may not be well with the circumstances of life, all is well with my soul. Through God's still, small voice, we can find ourselves in a thin place—a term used by ancient pagan Celts and later Christians, where the veil between this world and the eternal world is thin.

Frequently, the channel for finding that thin place is beauty. Even though my city view to the west is impeded, I get enough of a hint of sunset to remind me of my prairie childhood. There the sky was open and expansive, and the daily journey into dusk was a dose of the beauty of God. And it only takes a few bars of a cello playing before a tear quivers on my lashes, and I am rocketing towards that thin place.

Once from my office, I could hear a young child digging around in his locker while singing: *Jesus loves me this I know, for the Bible tells me so...* It was a beautiful sound. When I peeked to identify the singer, I had cause to pause and reflect. Here was a child who had tested the waters more than once in the past year and who came to us without a lot of church background. Yet his singing was so pure and sweet and clear that all of us in the office stopped to take note. A still, small voice was nudging his soul, and he was grasping the simple yet profound truth that Jesus loved him.

Years after my father's death, I heard a story about him that has profoundly affected me. My dad was an equal part farmer and musician, loving both the land and music. When he was nineteen, on the way home from his country church, his father passed the conducting baton over to him. That began a fifty-year service to choral music in congregations and many larger provincial church gatherings where music was the focus.

One evening, the Mennonite Historical Society in Saskatchewan honoured three conductors, all no longer with us, who had made significant contributions to music-making in the province. My dad was on that list. It was a lovely evening, with many significant people in our family's life all in one room. The visiting continued long into the evening when a small group of friends came over for a cup of tea. It was then I heard this story for the first time:

My dad regularly took part in the Mennonite Festival Chorus that sang with various conductors, including the renowned Robert Shaw. One winter, the chorus had the privilege of singing Beethoven's *Missa Solemnis* with Shaw in Toronto at Roy Thompson Hall. The discriminating crowd would appreciate this incredibly difficult music. Sitting backstage before the performance, my dad confessed his anxiety to the tenor beside him, who was now my storyteller. My dad was, after all, "just a farmer," and here he sat in this great music hall, singing this magnificent work, with a conductor for whom he had tremendous respect. In a word, he felt unworthy. His companion took one look at Dad's music, dog-eared and underlined from a long winter of diligently practicing on his own on the farm, looked him in the eyes and said, "This is a place where you belong."

At the end of the concert, many choir members were visiting and reliving what had been a tremendous musical and spiritual experience. Someone looked back toward the stage, and with others following their gaze, all discussion stopped. The choir was gone, the orchestra was gone, the audience was filing out. But there, sitting alone in the choir loft absorbing every last minute of the experience, was my dad. I surmise he didn't want to leave that thin place. I am sure that in that choir loft, the still small voice was so resonating in his heart and soul that he couldn't leave for the glory. A camera came out, and the moment was captured. I would pay a million dollars to see that picture.

The mystery of our God is unfathomable. His voice is like a mic that calls out even when it's supposedly not on. Its melodious sound escapes the lips of a boy at his locker. It beats in the heart of a farmer in a royal hall. And it's evident in the openness of even our youngest children. One Easter, our Kindergarten teacher was showing a video reenactment of Jesus's death on the cross. Suddenly, a small girl, pigtails flying and tears streaming, pushed through her classmates to her teacher. Her teacher enfolded her in her arms and brushed a tear away. "What's wrong?" Choking out the words, the young girl asked, "He did that for me?" There was perhaps no holier moment in school that year than this moment—a child grasped the enormity of God's love. The great mystery was unfurling to her through a still, small voice. It calls for you as well. Put on your mantle and stand in the presence of the One who calls you Beloved in a still, small voice.

CHAPTER 10
THE OPPORTUNITY OF CONFLICT

Seek peace and pursue it. (1 Peter 3:11)

Through the windows, the afternoon sunlight was meandering in and out of the clouds, but the boys in our meeting room were mainly looking at their feet. I knew that a summons to my office wasn't their idea of a happy afternoon, but it was vital that we talk. I called them together because one in their midst wasn't feeling connected, not part of the group, not happily throwing the football at recess. Such was his distress that his mother had quietly come to me and said they were considering other schools to give him a fresh start. I talked to the lad and poked around for hints from his teachers, but it seemed that this was a situation we needed to hash out. These boys had been happy together for seven years. It caught me by surprise that there was this level of hurt.

And so I started to prod them. What was going on? The boy with the wound talked about being a solitary moon, orbiting the planet the rest were on. He spoke of disconnect, discomfort, and a simmering distrust. To their credit, his peers listened, and then one of them blurted, "Yah, but you can be *so* annoying." My breath caught, and I wondered how this would land, but there was a nodding of heads and a smattering of examples offered quite factually. And then a turning point I couldn't have predicted came. The boy with the wound chuckled, actually chuckled, and admitted, "Yup, I can be like that." The tension eked out of the room.

I was no longer needed, so I just sat back and watched. Having owned his part of the story, everyone else felt free to do the same. They talked about what had been happening, how they could move on, and they sorted out how to proceed should more annoying things happen on either end. Most of all, there was relief in the room, getting this out in the open and restoring a relationship. In fact, days later, when I was hanging out after school in the atrium, one of the boys came up to me with an update and said, "Hey, it's going really well; we're all really trying." I couldn't ask for anything more.

I have to say this particular situation was an aberration. It stood out as a shining example of how things can quickly move forward with a recipe of honesty, willingness, and responsibility. I sat in that back-room meeting spot, sometimes daily, definitely weekly. The composition of people changed—the situations were all unique, but the issues at heart were very similar. A breach had occurred. People weren't seeing things the same. Something was simmering, causing hurt. And rarely, rarely, was the response to such disparity a chuckle and an admission of owning a part of the story. Far too often, defensiveness took the lead, justification sprung through crackles of pain, or even worse, an unwillingness to talk and address the situation surfaced. Silence and dismissal of others' perspectives robbed opportunities to change the scene from hurt to healing, from betrayal to shaky steps towards trusting again. Refusing to see and hear another side only creates a selfish, island pillar that bleeds rapidly out of the spirit of community. Our best hope is to intervene sooner with an authentic heart and a willingness to see resolution, giving up the hardline position of being right.

On more than one occasion, parents told me of their dismay in finding conflict in our Christian school. They had expected more. My response was always that we hoped for more, but any Christian community is also a slice of life in a broken world. When we come together with our backgrounds, experiences, opinions, and expectations, we are bound to rub up against others with different viewpoints. That doesn't

> To pursue PEACE is to remember our words and RESPONSES as we turn each corner of this fragmented LIFE.

mean we don't strive for a peaceable kingdom. Our grounding scripture verse of "Seek peace and pursue it" (1 Peter 3:11) was evidence that we knew we had work to do—to *pursue* that world where the lion rests by the lamb. To pursue is to be relentless, to keep moving forward, to pick oneself up over and over and keep trying to hit the mark. To pursue peace is to remember our words and responses as we turn each corner of this fragmented life. In fact, through a great deal of thought and deliberation, we created a PEACEMAKERS acronym, outlining what we wanted to strive for. I think I will be able to recite it by memory until the day I die.

> **P**—Participants
> **E**—Enthusiastic
> **A**—Accepting
> **C**—Christ-like
> **E**—Encouraging
> **M**—Mentors
> **A**—Aspiring
> **K**—Kind
> **E**—Excellent
> **R**—Responsible
> **S**—Servants

We had a beautiful wooden sign fashioned with these words and put it in a prominent place, with little replicas in every classroom. They were our sign on the doorpost to say, in this place, we strive to act with these values and goals. We talked about every letter of that acronym in chapels. I saw teachers lead their classes straight from the playground to that large sign, sit them down and say, "What I saw on the playground is not what we are about. Remember who you are, where we are, and how we act toward each other." It was significant learning not of subject curriculum but life curriculum. In my mind, it was the most important work we did. Year after year we presented a PEACEMAKERS award at the end of the year. I heard teachers tell the students, "This is the most important part of our school." Our entire teaching staff felt a hitch in their hearts when one of our valedictorian's final words to her classmates was, "Go from this place and be PEACEMAKERS." That this was their final message that they took from our collective space was a moment of satisfaction.

But at its very heart, PEACEMAKERS was not a program. It was a vision. It was a burning light we hoped everyone in our community latched on to, to carry as a guide for each moment of our days.

When the devastation of 9-11 happened, we were in our second week of school in our new building. At the same time that teachers and parents came through our doors and updated me on the horror unfolding through terrorism, ironically, our PEACEMAKERS sign was being hung. As it took its place of prominence, my spirit stirred with a huge thought: We could change the world. Crazy, I know, but everything on that sign was the polar opposite to what was happening in New York City. It showed a different way of being and living, inspired by what we felt Jesus was teaching us.

And what if? What if every student who came through our doors so absorbed each descriptor of the PEACEMAKERS acronym, they lived it out in their life? It would not only influence what happened in our hallways and playgrounds but also what our students carried out into the neighbourhoods and workplaces they found themselves in. And dare we hope that these children would go into all their future arenas with the influence of peace in their conversations, their communities, and even their conflicts? What if we sent out two hundred students each year determined to be PEACEMAKERS in every way they could? What if only one of them picked it up as a vibrant concept stirring in their heart and soul? It could happen. At the very least, we could change our corner of the world.

The very fact that we needed that program acknowledged that life wouldn't always hit that mark. It took work. It wasn't an expectation we always reached. It took learning and relearning to know what it meant to be a faithful steward in God's kingdom.

You probably recall a familiar, ancient Indian parable about the blind men and the elephant. A group of blind men who have never seen an elephant describe it from the specific part they touch. To one, it's a tusk, another a tail; to one, it's an ear, a trunk, or a broad, wrinkly side. Each of their definitions is only a small part of the whole. It's accurate but not complete. The more I worked with students, parents and teachers, boards and committees—yes, also the more I looked into my soul—the more I felt we were often stuck in our private description of the elephant and unwilling or unable to see that this was only one part. In fact, our dogmatism that our view of the elephant is actually the only part is what stops us from moving forward, from reconciling, from gaining perspective. It stops creativity in finding a forward-looking solution, and at its worst, it skids us off a path completely into unforgiving and unrelenting territory. It hurts community when we are right and alone, rather than open and somewhat brokenly together sharing our part of the picture. I have hung my head in dismay, watching as parts of the church hurt its people in the name of being righteously right. I have watched with humility as I saw people "of the world" lead only with kindness and with no expectation of reward.

One morning, I was in the gym with the Kindergarten class, supervising a rollicking game of frozen tag. Everyone was running and dodging and freezing; each knew their part and their expectation.

Some workers came in the outdoor side door, unobtrusively moving some equipment to the gym stage. One young boy took note, however, of this interruption to our happy camaraderie. He came next to me and, without a word, took my hand. We watched the game and the workers. We didn't speak, but we were intimately communicating with every breath. When he felt at peace again, ascertaining that no danger was impeding our little world, he gave my hand a quick squeeze and took off, into the fray of the game and the fray of life.

That's my hope for community. It's busy and productive and often fun. We're running together haphazardly with great purpose. Sometimes, little hints of danger or even big hints come our way. We can choose to disrupt the whole game of life happening around us, or we can connect, reaching out a hand deliberately where we need to, keeping the bond strong, warm, and safe until we have it figured out. It's imperative to living together. And then let's run back. Run into the game of life with open hearts, with a squeeze of the hand, each knowing our blissful part in building a kingdom that is bigger together than we ever can imagine alone. The elephant has many parts if we look deliberately at its big, ungainly, and beautiful whole. Be at peace.

CHAPTER 11
SOMETHING BEAUTIFUL IS HAPPENING HERE

He hath made everything beautiful in its time: also he hath set eternity in their heart, yet so that man cannot find out the work that God hath done from the beginning even to the end. (Ecclesiastes 3:11, ASV)

It was early on a school day, and I opened my eyes, reluctant to leave the warmth and calm of bed and to enter into the day's exuberance. Out my west-facing windows, I could see sunlight glimmering. The tops of trees were starting to reflect early morning rays. Turning over, coming in through the east bedroom window and in my hallway was the day's first light, a shimmering reflection against the wall. *Something beautiful is happening,* I thought, *but I can't quite see what it is.* I pushed myself out from under the covers and walked to the large east window in the back room. Leaving that comfort and safety, shivering a bit, was all worth it because when I could fully look east, my vision was no longer limited. Before me in glorious expanse was the sunrise—brilliant, deep colours emerging over treetops and the sleeping city.

Teachers throw out metaphors about participating with parents in the raising of children all the time. Frequently, we talk about planting seeds. In the year students are in our classroom, we have a chance to plant ideas, talk about character growth, grasp the teachable moment for all it's worth, and push a child a bit down a road they are scared and simultaneously eager to travel. And then we give them up—to the next grade, the next school, usually unsure what became of them or what kind of plant they flourished into. In our school, we had many kids who stayed with us for ten years, and that perspective was often rewarding. But time wasn't necessarily a measure of influence. Some students spent one short year with us, and the child we ushered into the doors in September changed remarkably when they sprinted down the stairs in June, confident and assured. And some students spent forever with us and somehow crashed and burned. And sometimes to our dismay, they left early, disgruntled and discontent. It stung when reconciliation didn't inch its way into our shared journey. We prayed to see glimpses of the sunrise, hoping for a peek of its brilliance, or we knew something beautiful was going on, but it wasn't ours to observe.

There are so many images of beautiful beginnings in our students where words are inadequate to describe the surprise and delight at catching even a glimpse. For example:

When I ushered a new student out at recess to join a kick-ball game, I watched with him on the sideline until I thought he was catching on to the arc of the game. When I encouraged him to take a turn and step up to the home plate, he looked terrified. The first two rolled pitches went right by him while he stared uncomprehendingly at the ball, and he didn't even attempt to kick the third pitch until it was already ringing off the backstop. He was swinging at air. Okay, so sports weren't going to be this kid's jam, but in a few years, when he was the lead in the musical and completely confident with complex dance steps, the light in his eyes started to shimmer.

One of our oldest teens checked out in June and totally bombed all his final exams. Yet he stood on stage at a graduation ceremony he had barely eked his way into and sang so beautifully there wasn't a dry eye in the house. He'd found his light, and it was glimmering.

There was a young student who, to her teacher's dismay, despite intensive help, only clicked into reading the last week of June. But she could, alternatively, be so mesmerized by placing blocks into intricate street patterns that a career in city design was only a flickering beam away.

An awkward volleyball player lingered after practice so that her coach could show her one more time how to get her serve over the net.

While they hung out in the gym, her serve sailed closer and closer each week until timing, hand-eye coordination, and dogged determination vaulted her into being the clutch server on the team. It was an eye-blink later that she stood confidently on a court as a university student and, in looking into the stands, caught the eye of her Junior High coach, who still supported the flame burning in her.

When the last day of school in June came each year, I stood in the atrium, saying goodbye to kids and parents. It was like being in a fast-flowing river stream fly fishing. I caught a backpacked kid on their way by, gave them a hug and released them into the summer and, in some cases, the rest of their lives. Sometimes they took a last look, sometimes they just barreled right out, but their teachers' gaze always lingered as the atrium emptied. The glimmers we had seen in our students' lives would blossom into a full sunrise just around a corner we weren't going to be able to observe. We lingered because it was our last glimpse of their potential, but it wasn't the final light display for those who had been entrusted briefly to us.

I sometimes wonder if the disciple Thomas's relationship with Jesus isn't an example for all of us in glimpsing the rays of the sunrise but not seeing the full view. I've always felt that the church associates the word "doubting" with derision affixed to Thomas, as if his doubt casts an aspersion on him as a faithful, committed disciple. However, I feel that Thomas's doubting made him into a thinking disciple. He wanted a relationship. He wanted desperately to believe. We know he was willing to follow Jesus to die with him (John 11:16). But Thomas also wanted an intimate experience with Jesus. After the pain of the crucifixion, Thomas wanted to touch Jesus's wounds, to feel the rent side of his flesh. He wanted to know not just intellectually but with his being—with his touch—that Jesus was real and alive and walking amidst them. That's a category we all should be in—to so long for the divine that we beg and plead to see the realness of our risen Lord. And what did Jesus do? I see no derision in his tone, no anger vibrating between them. Jesus wishes Thomas wouldn't need such proof, but the Master is willing to meet his disciple where he is at. Jesus came to him personally so that in response, Thomas could say, *"My Lord and my God!"* (John 20:28).

It is thought that Thomas would take that experience and become a missionary building the church. We need to give our children and young people that same opportunity: to see and experience the risen Lord in ways that are rich and meaningful to them—so we can send them on their way for greater kingdom work. To hear them utter, "My Lord and my God." By showing our students these rays of the rising sun, we show them a path to the kingdom, even when we have seen them exit the doors of our shared space where they will see a full sunrise beyond our vision.

At times one specific adult is responsible for spurring on a child—a coach who consistently sends a player on to the court with his arm around them and an encouraging word; a teacher who sits in a desk beside their uncomprehending student night after night to explain a complex algorithm; a teacher who kept an eye out for those who needed special accommodations in learning and playing, helping them taste success in a way they never thought they could. But often it's a whole gaggle that shuffles a child along, year after year.

We had one Grade one student who needed a relay team to get him onto the bus. On his own he couldn't manage—his backpack spilled with uneaten snacks and pesky important papers leaking from partially closed zippers. He was inevitably late and increasingly anxious about missing the bus. You could see the fear in his eyes, some imagined scenario that he would be on the sidewalk alone, far from home. So his Grade one teacher got him together as best she could amidst her other charges and handed him off to me. I was his escort through the chaotic throngs of others in the hallway and down the steps to the bus, picking up the debris that escaped from his bag on the way. I handed him off to the kind bus driver who greeted him cheerfully and placed this young boy on the seat behind him where he could keep an eye on him. And finally, a grateful mother waited at the bus stop to collect her boy, who, with all the odds not against him but in his favour, made it intact. At each stage, this young boy locked eyes with the person who would help him next on that particular stage of the journey. He locked eyes and trusted that he would get to the next place safely. And that trust got him to the next step, and the next, until he was home. It's the only way to go through life, to feel confident enough in travelling the journey together, sometimes only metres at a time, but knowing that you have a cloud of witnesses to get you through that stage until you reach your heavenly home where the Master is waiting.

This winter, a former Kindergarten teacher from our school, also an accomplished artist, received a unique invitation. A student contacted her to see if her teacher of decades past would contribute artwork to her personal show. And one of the pieces already hanging? A framed picture that was created in Kindergarten by the artist as a five-year-old, under the direction of one with a shared love for colour, creativity, and design which inspired her to put paint to paper then and now. It boggles the mind. The hints of light that began in that Kindergarten class refracted into many sacred, shimmering slivers in two lives. And it was only when a corner, years in the making was turned, that the full glory was visible. Something beautiful was happening, and we didn't know it. But the One who calls us Beloved could see it coming all along. He is the divine Creator who paints a picture for us in the heavens each morning and night, which sparks beauty within us all.

CHAPTER 12
OBEY HIS VOICE, BE HIS PEOPLE

You shall put these words of mine in your heart and soul, and you shall bind them as a sign on your hand, and fix them as an emblem on your forehead. Teach them to your children, talking about them when you are at home and when you are away, when you lie down and when you rise. Write them on the doorposts of your house and on your gates, so that your days and the days of your children may be multiplied in the land that the Lord swore to your ancestors to give them, as long as the heavens are above the earth. (Deuteronomy 11:18–21)

It was a pandemic dream that woke me. I had been wandering invisibly through buildings. Literally. Passing straight through a wall and observing what was going on then moving to the next.

On my last visit before jolting back into the land of the living, I came to a church. It wasn't one I was familiar with. It had a modern edge to it, with plush seating in a large auditorium sanctuary. A great crowd was standing, shoulder to shoulder, and singing in beautiful harmony, "Guide me O, Thou Great Jehovah."

The song tugged at my soul. During these long months of isolation and online church viewing, I missed singing the most. Who could have predicted that at some point, singing would be a forbidden activity? So I revelled in the beauty of the old, familiar hymn.

Then something struck me as if I had forgotten the danger of the present reality: this congregation wasn't socially distanced. They were packed in! Against the pandemic rules! They were singing! Against the pandemic rules!

Now that I had this information, what would I do? Would I report them? Would I pass invisibly through to the next building and keep observing? Would I tap a leader on the shoulder and point out the infraction? When I awoke, my mind was spinning with the connections between rules and living together freely.

The Israelites, who are often referred to as a "stubborn people" (Deuteronomy 9:13), had difficulty adapting to rules. They heard God's voice give them the Ten Commandments. Yet, while Moses was with God on the mountain for forty days and nights, they grew restless. With Aaron, they built a golden calf to worship. Even having been part of the divine revelation, it didn't stick with them.

When Moses returned to the scene of their disobedience around a golden calf, he was so angry that he flung down the tablets and broke them. He had to return to God and plead for mercy for the people. He and God reforged the Ten Commandments, and after another forty days and nights, Moses returned to the stiff-necked people and went about teaching them… repeatedly.

Moses was the wise and fervent intermediary between God and his people, the teacher of the people who needed repeated lessons, admonitions, and the wisdom of a lion-hearted leader. Getting the people to the Promised Land didn't require just one Red Sea miracle. The journey required a weaving, difficult path with daily intervention of manna, frequent resetting of the trail, forgiveness from flagrant disobedience, and mercy. Always, mercy.

It's not a bad mantra for how we get through life together. A school needs rules to make it from September to June in some orderly fashion. But too many rules and details bogs everyone down in the minutia. It's better to paint broad strokes that define learning and living than setting out too many regulations.

When Jesus came, and the Pharisees tried to pin him down about the most important commandment, he reduced everything to two things: love the Lord your God with all your heart, and with all your soul, and with all your mind. And love your neighbour as yourself (Matthew

22:37–39). Then, like Moses, Jesus went about teaching, pointing people in the direction they should go, and showing mercy.

Nothing becomes perfect through rules alone. These are only a part of the journey, which requires a continued, precious combination of teaching and mercy. Rules are our guidelines, but love is the glue that keeps us connected on our shared path, especially when we stumble. When things inevitably go wrong, we revisit mercy and teaching.

We had a family at our school that spent most of their summer at a northern lake. Inevitably, they squeezed every moment out of the long summer days and came screeching back to the city just before school started. Predictably, the transition was rough. There wasn't time to recalibrate from long, lazy, carefree days to an environment dictated by the ring of a bell and a classroom or playground lineup that took you from spot to spot.

In the first hour of the first day, we always had a school assembly to gather our community for a shared blessing for the year. But for the oldest child of the family, this was an impossible moment. It was his first school experience, and he couldn't sit in that Kindergarten line on the gym floor. He was beyond squirrely; unable to contain himself, disrupting everyone.

I watched the situation out of the corner of my eye until the teacher wisely realized that this child wasn't going to settle. She scooped up this little tornado in her arms, and carried him squawking out of the gym. I remember his mother's rueful comment that this wasn't the way she had expected her family's schooling to start.

It got way better—without incident, really, but September was always bumpy. I encountered this same boy a few years later in the hallway. He should have been outside for recess, but he was straggling. As I made my way through the hallway, I threw an off-handed comment of, "You'd better get outside" in his direction.

His response, however, made me stop. "You," he declared, "are not the boss of me." Well, technically, I was, but he wasn't buying it. He wasn't going to speed up in any way, shape, or fashion to get outside other than his own sweet time. I watched him with a bit of amusement until he finally got outside, and when I saw his dad later that day, I relayed the anecdote with a wry smile. Dad, however, took it seriously.

While I don't know what went on at home that night, except that it was a long evening for everyone, a sheepish young lad handed me a paper the next day. It had lines written on it, over and over in varying Grade two lopsided printing sizes until the end of the paper. *You are the boss. You are the boss. You are the boss.* I accepted it graciously, but it wasn't long before the paper was taken off my desk—only to be returned later as a framed print. It hung in my office for years, not only as a conversation piece but as a reminder of the importance of balancing the dynamic between freedom and structure in the changing landscape of living together.

Child number two showed her displeasure for September and being in Kindergarten by having a mini-meltdown between the classroom and the gym each time the class made the short trip. At some point, in exasperation, the gym teacher just picked her up and carried her to the gym, hoping she would recalibrate once there. But this scenario continued until eventually, the teacher scooped up this sobbing, miserable kid and handed her off to me in my office. Child number two snuggled into my lap, content not to be in the gym. With a warm, sniffling bundle on my lap, I picked up the phone to call dad. I said to our girl that she would have to explain to her father why she wasn't in gym class. She nodded her head solemnly, took the receiver, and in the blink of an eye turned on the sweetest, most innocent voice and said, "Hi Daddy!" I rolled my eyes outwardly, but truly it was no hardship to sit with this curly headed girl in my arms while she chattered away.

I had a sense of déjà vu when child number three from this family was in Grade two, and I had a call from his teacher for help in her first week of school. There was child number three, somewhat ingeniously squished into an open shelf, refusing to come out, refusing to participate in regular school activity. He was finding the best way he could to not be in that classroom save bolting for home. I knew by now what was happening. Rules and regulations were overwhelming after summer. So I bent down and whispered, "Come with me," and I walked out of the classroom, happy that little feet were trailing after me. We'd get it sorted out. It required teaching. It required mercy. It required a growing balance of perspective on the tension between freedom and rules.

We all give up a little freedom to make the world operate. That's why driving in rush hour goes as well as it does. We agree implicitly and explicitly to obey the laws of the road. It's why most people complied during a pandemic—even about singing—for the general wellbeing of others, not just their own liberties.

But there is also something beautiful about moments of freedom, launching our own way, and expressing our hearts because our voice matters. It's kind of like getting a class from their homeroom to the gym. They line up at the door, walk single file to pass others in the hallway, stop in an orderly fashion for a drink, and finally get to the gym. Then they take off like a shot. They run and run, laughing and screaming and flailing their arms. It's utter abandon, sheer folly, pure joy. And finally, once that initial energy is expended, they drift to the circle to rejoin the class, hear the next directions, clarify the game's rules, and organize into teams. And then they move freely within those new parameters.

Our lives are like that, we the stiff-necked people of the kingdom of God. With the undergirding of love for God first and then our neighbour, we navigate the trails of our lives. It's a necessary part of our jobs, families, and churches. There are never straight lines. The way is long and winding, frequently difficult. It might require a miracle or the intervention of a wise saint, or we might collapse under unfortunate golden-calf disobedience along the way. But our God remains steadfast and true, and as we bask under our freedom and play in the lines to keep everyone safe, we negotiate the way together.

My school choir used to sing this beautiful promise from Jeremiah:

> *Obey my voice, and I will be your God,*
> *and you shall be my people,*
> *and walk only in the way that*
> *I command you,*
> *so that it may be well with you.* (Jeremiah: 7:23)

A pretty good payoff, don't you think? God's people walking the bumpy and unpredictable trail of life together, basking in the sun's warmth, singing his song, hearing his voice, lovingly called the children of God.

CHAPTER 13
STEPPING STONES IN THE STREAM OF LIFE

For the Lamb at the center of the throne will be their shepherd, and he will guide them to springs of the water of life, and God will wipe away every tear from their eyes.
(Revelation 7:17)

It was the only September in several decades that I wasn't in a school of some sort. My mind stayed in that familiar groove of the hectic pace of the first weeks when everyone was establishing routines and sorting out their place. But I was in the middle of a stream in eastern Australia. There were lovely tree-lined banks on the side of the stream with a well-worn path in the dappled sunlight to comfortably enjoy this slice of the world.

But the stream was also inviting. It wasn't particularly fast-moving, and there were many rocks protruding from the water, erratically spaced out and usually slippery, but my travelling companion and I had chosen to navigate this stream by hopping from stone to stone. This involved mapping out a course to avoid getting stuck, and certainly, there was the potential to fall and get wet. We took a risk. And the experience was exciting and adventuresome, and the time flew by.

Taking a break with a snack on a large rock and water lapping around us, I thought of kids across the world going to school right now. They were figuring out their lives, and it wasn't unlike this stream navigation. As a faith and education community, we provided them with the stepping stones to guide their life. Ultimately the path they chose was their own, and we were there as a support. They were plotting it out, moving from stone to stone. Here they chose a lifelong friend. Jump. Here they were piqued by a certain subject matter. Jump. Here their heart was stirred by the prompting of the Spirit to act with compassion. Jump. Each leap plotted their course. Some stones were pivotal, giving lasting direction. There were times they landed shakily and times when they fell off completely and got wet. Sometimes that was the wrong rock to choose altogether, and it just didn't work out. But another, steadier spot wasn't far away. Sometimes it needed to be pointed out. Sometimes it was just there for the leaping if they had the eyes to see.

Although having a full and deep appreciation for the public school system, I chose to spend most of my career in Christian education. I felt a call to provide teaching in informative subject matter and frame living and learning into the perspective of faith. With other like-minded parents and staff members, I wanted to bring kids directly into the flowing stream of life and point out the stepping stones they could centre their journey on.

Sometimes the stones we pointed out moved students so that they were against the current. In fact, there's mud at the bottom of a stream, and sometimes it needs to be acknowledged. For the most part, kids came to our school with good knowledge of the Bible and its stories. There were times, however, especially among our older students, where it was time to push back, to fling a little mud into their correct, easy-answer world. Because as you and I know, life's answers rarely come easily, and decisions that may seem easy when we gaze from a distance aren't nearly as easy when you are the person directly involved. Our children need to learn about accountability, but they also need to learn about grace—and for some reason, that was far more difficult. If their world became about opposites—black and white, righteous and unrighteous, Christian and non-Christian, us and them, their worldview became equally stark and uncompromising. Such a view negates our Lord, who ate with the tax collectors and touched the unclean. And so we pushed them. We asked, "Why do you think that way? What if you were in that position? Is there only one answer to this dilemma?" And soon, they couldn't just parrot phrases back at us. They had to wrestle with the issue for themselves.

Most importantly, they had to walk into that area of life that was grey and agonize over what isn't fair, or easy, or simple. A little mud had been flung.

It's one thing to try and shift our students' worldview to be more realistic and encompassing. However, some students are mired dangerously in the mud of the stream of life. We had an international student with us for a brief time. His English ability was limited, so it was hard to get a good sense of what he was comprehending in class or how he was adapting to Canada. Most of our international students were keen, eager, and worked hard on a tough path to improve their English skills and navigate their new cultural realities. This student seemed sullen, withdrawn, and morose. When the bricks tumbled to destruction, they tumbled hard and fast. A learning assistant noticed some dark and troubling illustrations in his work. With keen intuition, she brought it to our attention, and a number of us met with the student.

Haltingly, the story was pieced together. His life in his home country had been very difficult, and his single mother basically sent him away. He was now isolated and alone in his placement home in Canada. He was unstable and having shadowy, demonic hallucinations. He shifted between unknown, horrible, imagined worlds, surfacing only briefly into the present. Our hearts ached for this untethered, distraught youth unmoored from life, alone in almost every possible way, and really without a place in this world to go. We called immediately for professional intervention, and he was transported to the hospital, where he would stay for months under expert medical and psychological care. On our end, teachers stayed in touch providing schoolwork, and our kind and attentive learning assistant continued to work far beyond the call of duty, making frequent trips to the hospital to visit a boy who didn't have much to say. In reality, she was his lifeline. With unexpected compassion to one unresponsive to her efforts, she illuminated stepping stones one at a time that would help him ever so slowly move one foot at a time out of the mud.

If life isn't primarily about personal happiness but about personal transformation, there continues to be much to explore and learn. It's a growing awareness of which direction our lives are going. And because there will inevitably be hard spots, the wrestling with angels, the dark nights of the soul... there needs to be a centre, a grounding to keep our footing, our perspective, indeed, our faith.

It occurs to me that when we can shift the stream-navigating mindset to one where mud is part of living, we can also bring in the next stepping stone—a heart of compassion and mercy. In a me-first, win a trophy at every turn world, with hovering adults ready to intervene at the slightest misstep, our kids know they are important. And who can argue with healthy self-esteem and boosted confidence? But we go overboard when we neglect to teach our children to love their neighbours as themselves.

Usually, life circumstances are the best opportunities to teach compassion. In my final Grade one teaching year, I took my class on a field trip to see thirty thousand baby chicks. One of the accompanying mothers called early to say that she couldn't make it. She was seven months pregnant and wasn't feeling well. By 9:30 a.m., she was in the hospital, her blood pressure skyrocketing. By 2:00 p.m., they had performed an emergency C-section and sent a three-pound five-ounces baby girl to a hospital that specialized in premature babies. The danger for the mother didn't end. Her blood pressure was too high, and nothing they did could bring it down. She became bloated to the point that when her mother went to be with her, she couldn't recognize her daughter. At midnight, her husband stumbled home to get some rest. Half an hour later, the hospital called him back, unsure if his wife would make it through the next hour. Finally, at dawn, the crisis passed, although the situation was still critical. At my door at 8:30 was a gaunt and tired husband, bringing his six-year-old to school. He had lived an eternity the past day. I gladly took his daughter into the fold of our classroom to bring a little normalcy into her life.

For a week, both baby and mother struggled, taking one step forward and one step back. And in the halls outside my classroom, other parents pondered how they could help. And so we mobilized. For an entire week, the kids kept a secret from their classmate as they worked. They helped their parents shop for baby things. They baked cookies, and parents and teachers added casseroles, loaves of bread, and desserts to the pile. Mothers who sewed took doll patterns and made tiny clothes for a baby. Kids brought their allowances to school, and we bought books for their classmate, diapers for the baby, and bubble-bath for a tired mom. The kids wrote stories, letters, and fancy cards, and together we created a colourful banner to put in the baby's room.

When mom came home, we called her to school and placed boxes and boxes of things we had collected in front of her. It was one of those moments in life that defies words. The family was overwhelmed by what a class of six-year-olds had done. They returned to the NICU and told the nurses, "You'll never believe what happened…" But more importantly, my class had learned something I couldn't teach out of a book. They showed compassion and concern for people in need. Every day they asked about the baby, kept tabs on how she was growing and waited impatiently for the day—a month later—when she could come for "show and tell."

I can't think of a more important characteristic for our children than to look out from their small world with eyes of mercy. We need to look no further than Jesus as our example. At times, the disciples needed to row with Jesus out to sea so that he could escape the crowds. Imagine what his days were like—the people clamouring to be touched by his healing hand, to hear his wisdom, to be surrounded by his love. And what a wondrous love it was—for Matthew, Zacchaeus, Mary and Martha, and countless others—their lives would never be the same. If only we had a small portion of that compassion, one portion of his merciful kindness, the world would never be the same. Once we have experienced that love and compassion, and bring our children into these experiences, then a part of that life-giving love and mercy is in them as they carry the light of Christ within.

One busy day at school, it wasn't until just before the final bell that I finally made my daily rounds through classrooms. I walked into a primary room and meandered through the desks to see what they were up to when a boy looked up at me and said two words: "You're late." I was a bit blown away. Honestly, my presence was so routine I didn't think anyone noticed much when or if I came and went. But clearly, eyes were watching and noting. That's why the stepping stones we put into kids' lives are so important. They are always watching, learning, discerning, deliberating, and interpreting. In the important task of training up children in the ways of the Lord, we plant them by the stream of life. Let's be alert to the Holy Spirit, sensitive to the lives under our care, and in close touch with the Master we follow so that we all may walk in and towards the Eternal Light.

CHAPTER 14
WANDERER, COME HOME

*So he set off and went to his father. But while he was still
far off, his father saw him and was filled with compassion;
he ran and put his arms around him and kissed him.*
(Luke 15:20)

The first weeks of school are resplendently, exhaustingly busy. On top of that which beckoned us in the hubbub of those initial days, seasoned teachers kept an eye on the door. We waited to see which of our newly-minted alumni would return first. It happened every year. Someone who had moved on to high school was keen to come back, to check-in, to fill us in on how things were going in their new reality. They wanted their new story to be still connected to our story. It was always a moment of privilege to know that when they walked through our familiar doors and saw our faces, they felt at home.

We often connect home with a place and the people there. My heart hasn't stopped giving a bit of a tug when I crest the hill on a gravel road, where I can see the red barn of our farm in the distance. When I left home for the last time, I tried to memorize the imprint of my father walking the narrow path between that barn and the house, entering the kitchen to see my mother pulling bread out of the stove. They were the images of home.

When my office phone gave a short ring, I knew it was an internal call. I wondered which student might be in a pickle and making their way to see me. But the teacher on the other end was relaxed. One of her students hadn't returned from recess, and she wondered if I would round up the straggler. I checked the sunlit playground, peeked into washrooms, and started to pick up the pace when I couldn't find him in any common areas. I grabbed a couple of free adults, and we expanded the search, including every nook and cranny in the school. Soon we were moving into the neighbourhood, but when I had to grab my car keys to start a broader search, I knew we had to make two calls: the parents and the police. They converged quickly on our school.

It took us an additional endless hour to find our boy. It was an adult in a vehicle circling in wider and wider circles who eventually spotted him. He was wandering alone down a sidewalk, a decent distance away from school, in a direction he thought led towards home. He was excited about a new puppy in his neighbourhood and wanted to check on the acquisition. He thought that recess would be a good time to do that, oblivious to the chaos his departure had caused and to the quick mobilization of searchers.

I'm pretty sure I can accurately say: when his eyes connected at last with his family, when he was embraced into their fold, all that was home seeped around him to create a place of belonging. Somewhere in his bones, he knew that when he was lost, whether he was aware of it or not, those who loved him would keep circling until he was found.

The story of the Return of the Prodigal Son in Luke 15 is a familiar one. On the one hand, it's a story about choices and responses. The younger son thought he knew what was best and squandered his inheritance, only to realize he'd made a huge mistake later. He had sense enough, though, to humble himself when he hit rock bottom and go where he was unconditionally loved. We all know that place—it's called home. His response when getting there was immediate: he acknowledged the wrong he had done and asked for forgiveness. The father's choice was instinctive; he forgave his son even before his confession. His love was unconditional.

This story involves one more player who had to make a choice, the oldest son. I used to think that the older son got short-changed in the story. He'd been faithful to his father, stuck around, and did his duty without fanfare. And now, not only is the uncalled for celebration for his wayward brother going on, but no one even bothered to call him in from the field to include him. It seems that righteous indignation is called for.

But here is the issue. Yes, he did many things right in being a conscientious elder son. But his heart wasn't open enough to forgive. His arms didn't open to embrace. His soul didn't respond with compassion. The older son made a bad decision in his response. At best, he was narrow-minded; at worst he was self-centred and judgmental. The older brother thought this was about him and what he deserved. It wasn't. It was about his ability to rejoice over the one who has been lost, the ability—or lack thereof—to reach beyond himself. In fact, the father goes to both of his sons to welcome them into his life. The distance wasn't with the young, wayward son. The cold shoulder came from the older son, who was the one removed from the heart of life. Although physically present in his father's house, he was distant and cold.

It's not a stretch to think of the father figure as God. God's love is unconditional. God is always waiting expectantly for us. We cannot go where he is not. We cannot do anything bad enough that would separate us from him. We may leave God, but he will never leave us. His embrace is open, his attitude forgiving, and his ability to rejoice in those he loves is endless.

If I have to identify with the brothers, I'm more concerned about my older brother tendencies than my younger brother tendencies. The one thing the younger brother had going for him was an awareness of how far he had left home—physically and spiritually. The older brother was at home, yet far away.

How often have we within the church hurt others with our resentment, judgment, and condemnation? What happens when those in the church who are so rightly concerned about avoiding sin bring indignation and self-service to our gatherings of celebration? Are we resentful that grace is given to those we feel are less deserving? Might we be startled to know that God isn't only looking for those who are lost? He is also looking for those lingering on the inside with the wrong mindset.

I now look back at prodigal stories that grew out of my school, uncertain who the lesson was for. Waiting outside my office for me one morning was a father and his wayward son. They were close friends of a current school stalwart family. Through that connection and recommendation, I'd agreed to talk. It was our second meeting to discern whether our school community was a fit for their family. The youth was reluctant—to put it mildly. He had been involved with drugs in his last school and wasn't interested in being in a small church-affiliated school. But I had been insistent that if he were to come and be with us, I wanted a commitment in letter format that he would abide by the parameters that governed our learning and living. A fresh start was offered, but expectations were in place.

If you think this story is going in the direction of sudden transformation, you'd be wrong. I couldn't say that our school had a huge impact on that boy. He came reluctantly but not morosely; he was undoubtedly successful in making friends and completing requirements. His teachers enjoyed and encouraged his unique perspective on life. When he moved on to High School, there were other bumps and a return to his darker side. He caused a few grey hairs in his parents' lives. But, much like the circling van looking for a lost boy, love always chased after him. In no small part due to this and his strength and fortitude, he found his way quite brilliantly.

Also, through that decision to accept that family into our community came huge unanticipated bonuses for those of us who weren't initially the main player. Through their professional expertise, both parents plugged into areas that we were lacking and filled a void. Further siblings joined the school and brought delight. Lifelong friendships developed, not only between students but between adults.

Can you see how lines are blurred? How each of us drifts into the role of the lost prodigal or distant brother? How we don't stand with arms wide enough and our hearts lack compassion? Can you see how many dots God has connected to bring transformation beyond our wildest imagination to those who don't even know they are in the story? This story isn't just about a boy with a letter, but a pursuing, patient God involved in the whole dramatic picture, keenly going to each person, inviting them to be part of his kingdom work, to leave our lost ways, to leave our judgmental attitude, and, finally, to embrace the joy of living in community.

No matter what circumstances unfold, someone is circling at breakneck speed for the lost. That is the place where family, church, and the school find common ground. We are at our best when these institutions work together. We have a higher calling: to point our children and young people to our eternal home where God beckons, calling us, saving us a spot at the banquet table he has thrown in our honour.

> No matter what CIRCUMSTANCES unfold, someone is CIRCLING at breakneck speed for the LOST.

No author has influenced me more than Henri Nouwen in how he establishes the warmth and depth of the relationship of the Father, Son, and Holy Spirit and the children of God. It is a startling intimacy that has captured my soul. And I'm inspired to impart it to those God has placed in my path. Listen to Nouwen's words in his last published book before his death:

> Let us focus our eyes on the road we are travelling as we move forward, step by step, to our goal. We will encounter great obstacles and splendid views, long, dry deserts and also freshwater lakes surrounded by shadow-rich trees. We will have to fight against those who try to attack and rob us. We also will make wonderful friends. We will often wonder if we will ever make it, but one day we will see coming to us the One who has been waiting for us from all eternity to welcome us home. Yes, we can drink our cup of life to the bottom, and as we drink it we will realize that the One who has called us "the Beloved" even before we were born, is filling us with everlasting life.[5]

Let's get in our vehicles and circle around as we pursue our children and young people with relentless love, recognizing that God does the

---

[5] Henri Nouwen, *Can You Drink the Cup?* (Notre Dame: Ave Maria Press, 2012), 102.

same for us. You are called Beloved. A spot in eternity is waiting for you, held by none other than the Great I Am, who anticipates your arrival. Come home, dear wanderer, come home. All that is home is seeping around you to create a place in which you belong.

CHAPTER 15
UNUSUAL KINDNESS

*After we had reached safety, we then learned that the
island was called Malta. The natives showed us unusual
kindness.* (Acts 28:1–2)

In the months winding down my job in a country school and preparing to move about six hours away to a city school, an interesting
dinner helped push me to the transition. Ironically, a board member
from the city school that had recently hired me worked in oil and gas
and had to check on oil wells close to my country school. Although
we'd never met, Reg took the initiative to call and asked if I'd be open
to having dinner with him one evening while he was in my area. The
distance between the oil wells, my school and the place we could meet
for dinner was significant. Yet, Reg insisted on driving to my school
after his workday and picking me up, driving me to dinner, driving me
back to my car at the school. As the final rays of the sunset were fading,
he would have to drive again to return to his accommodation, making
it a long day for him. But I sensed no burden from him; in fact, the
extra miles were a joyful opportunity for conversation.

Our dinner together was heartfelt and gracious. We talked about
our dreams for this fledgling school and the lives we could touch. Questions I had were fielded, and I started to feel a simmering excitement
for what lay ahead. Through sharing a bit of my country story, I also
felt that there was a genuine interest to understand me and the context
I was coming from. (It was also a detail he never forgot. Years later, he
would bring me a book that featured my hometown that he found in a
secondhand store. There was a twinkle in his eye as he passed it along

to me, knowing it would tug at my heart.) It also brought me a sense of comfort, knowing that where I was going was filled with good people with warm hearts and big dreams.

In retrospect, this dinner was an unusual kindness. A new teacher isn't a big deal in a school; it happens every year. And there were no guarantees that I would be a good fit or last any longer than the year. I wasn't a good investment yet, but he invested anyway. And being on the board was a volunteer opportunity—not his main job—yet Reg approached it with an equal conviction and sincerity as he gave to checking out his oil wells. The many ways he'd gone out of his way to make this happen so stayed with me that when some three-plus decades later, Reg's life was unexpectedly taken, this lovely evening was the first memory that came to mind.

In the last chapter of Acts, Paul and his fellow prisoners and their captors landed on the Island of Malta after a dramatic shipwreck. Their number was large—276 people were on the ship, and they had been without food for a time. Their emotions were many: fear for their safety, hunger and illness from their ordeal, fatigue from the storm, worry for the unknown. Yet they jumped ship—some swimming, some gripping onto planks from the ship—and through God's grace, they made it to shore. Wet, bedraggled, and anxious, the prisoners gasped their way, not knowing what to expect. How would they be received? Most of them were prisoners, a motley and dangerous crew, and some soldiers whose main goal was to deliver the prisoners to Rome safely; otherwise, they would also be killed.

What would you do if you were on the island receiving these unwanted guests? Barricade them? Confine them to the beach? Hide the women and children? Tell the crew they have twenty-four hours to leave? It only takes us two verses in Chapter 28 to get to the heart of the matter. Of all things, the natives of Malta showed those shipwrecked "unusual kindness" (Acts 28:2). Fires warmed them from the rain and cold. They were entertained hospitably. And, startlingly, many honours were bestowed upon them. When they sailed again, provisions were placed on board (Acts 28:2–10). These dregs on society's chain were treated with dignity and benevolence.

We learn a fierce lesson from the natives of Malta. Their immediate response was unusual kindness, behaviour that honoured human life, regardless of the shipwrecked persons' background or sin. With the warmth of fire, food, and shelter, how many lives were saved? How many were potentially transformed? I'm touched that they responded simply with the necessities of life. They didn't psychoanalyze, condemn, or offer to build long-term huts where they could stay and live. They basically said, while you are here among us, we will treat you with love and grace. They followed the advice of novelist Henry James: "Three things in human life are important. The first is to be kind. The second is to be kind. And the third is to be kind."[6]

We once had a young student at our school plagued with ichthyosis, sometimes known as fish scale disease. The skin throughout her body constantly hardened and shed. Although her mother went to extreme lengths to dress her daughter beautifully, to stylishly comb her hair and place it in barrettes, it wasn't easy to see past the unremitting shedding of her skin. To sit in a desk side by side with her, meant skin flecks fell on your books. To hold hands in a group game meant holding a crackling hand that left its skin debris in yours. To hug her at the end of the day meant brushing off your clothes from what lingered. Repeatedly, bloody cracks would form on her body and Band-Aids were needed to bind the wound throughout the week. It was, sadly, off-putting for her peers. But of greater consequence, it was an unrelenting reality for her—living with a condition she couldn't alter or change, resulting in frustration and acting out from her isolation with this deck of cards life handed her.

What could be altered and changed were our attitudes. I saw it slowly happen as children more frequently chose compassion. Gentle souls shared their things with her in the classroom. A group of girls engaged her in their games on the playground. A deep breath was taken, and excess skin debris was pushed aside off the painting table. But perhaps the unusual kindness came from the girl herself, as she once again waited for people to adjust, accept, and see past the outward flaking shell to the tenderness of her heart and soul. I wonder if she is still fighting that battle—wishing that people would respond first and foremost with

---

[6] Attributed to Henry James, Public Domain.

kindness instead of awkwardness or distaste. I wonder if the lesson to learn was more ours than hers: be kind, be kind, be kind.

What does a world look like where unusual kindness is our first response? I've seen it often. It was the parent who planted a bed of one hundred tulips in the fall to delight us with their arrival in spring. It was the grandparent who spent days building an intricate set design for the school play. It was the Grade nine buddy who scooped up his Grade one charge, who was hurt and crying on the playground and brought her into the school for a Band-Aid. It was the coach who hung around well past the allotted time for a parent to pick up a player from a game using the time to connect and talk. It was a volunteer school librarian who not only sorted books and told stories but brought in chocolate chip cookies for teachers each library day. It was an unexpected coffee on a desk, a pot of soup for a struggling family, a note of encouragement at exactly the right time.

We can't forget these experiences of unexpected kindness. They will be forever etched in our minds. They may have been kind words in dark moments, an action that went way beyond what was expected, an unwavering support through a difficult time. Those acts of kindness become lifelines and frequently propel us to a different trajectory.

How do we intervene with unusual kindness in our own small and insignificant lives or when strangers land on our shores? The same Paul who was shipwrecked in Malta writes later in Galatians about how we are to treat each other. *"The fruit of the Spirit is love, joy, peace, patience, kindness, generosity, faithfulness, gentleness and self-control"* (Galatians 5:22–23). This is followed a few verses later by the words: *"Bear one another's burdens and in this way you will fulfill the law of Christ"* (Galatians 6:2).

Who will land on your shore? Who will arrive bedraggled and wet, anxious about how you will respond? You can choose to bear another's burdens and show them unexpected kindness. You will have opportunities to show love, joy, and peace. You have it in you to react with patience and gentleness. You may have the occasion to be generous to a fault with a lovely conversation over dinner and a drive. And through your unusual kindness, a journey will become easier, a burden lightened, a difficult day made more bearable. It will be easier for someone to take the next step in their journey. And you will be the hands and feet of Christ as we walk together in kingdom ways toward his ever-present light.

CHAPTER 16

CARRYING A HEAVY LOAD

Come to me, all you that are weary and are carrying heavy burdens, and I will give you rest. Take my yoke upon you, and learn from me; for I am gentle and humble in heart, and you will find rest for your souls. For my yoke is easy, and my burden is light. (Matthew 11:28–30)

Before my summer job started and my last year of Education studies began, I was home on the farm for a few weeks. My dad had sent me with a full load of seed grain to the land farthest from our home. He would follow with the tractor and seeder. The grain truck I drove was new to our farm fleet, with a split-shift transmission I hadn't used. I had a brief training session on how to use the red button beside the stick-shift to shift to an intermediary stage between the main gears. My twenty minutes of training had been on a flat stretch with an empty load. Now I had to drive a heavy load down into the valley of our small town and up a long, steady series of hills to our land. I admit being nervous about that red button and my ability to manage it, but when I got to the last and the longest hill I convinced myself that I was almost home free if I could reach the crest. I also thought that if I picked a slow and steady gear on the lower part where shifting was easy, it would get me to the top, and I wouldn't have to try the red button business on the incline.

Wishful thinking. Admittedly, I was close. I was almost at the top when it became clear that the gear I had chosen wasn't going to do the trick. I panicked when I heard the engine sputter—should I shift the wobbly stick-shift I knew how to use down? Should I engage that darn red button? Maybe I would miraculously make it? While I was madly considering my options, the engine died. It couldn't have been a worse spot. If I'd had time to look around, the high viewpoint was pretty—rolling prairie hills dotted with crocuses, meadowlarks on fence posts singing their eloquent song, wispy clouds in an endless, sun-bright sky. But instead, I was laser-focused on the dashboard and the engine light. Acting on instinct, I rammed my foot onto the clutch to restart the truck. Of course, when I engaged the clutch, I started rolling backwards. So I turned and reefed and twisted on that ignition key desperate to get going again—until I ripped the key! I kid you not—there was a tear right through the metal. Such is the strength of sheer panic. So there I was, rolling backwards to certain, utter catastrophe. What would happen if I crashed to the bottom, with a truck that I could no longer start and the weight of a full load gaining speed? The silence was deafening. Even the meadowlarks were without song.

Help arrived suddenly and precipitously from the opposite direction in a rickety half-ton and a plume of dust along the grid road. A farmer heading to the elevators in town pulled up alongside me. He was going forward, and I was still going backward. How I was steering that backward moving truck to stay on the road, I have no idea. The farmer rolled down his window and, ever the friendly country neighbour, he didn't skip the pleasantries. "Hi!" he said. I greeted him back, but there was sheer terror on my face. "What's wrong?" he asked. "I'm stalled and rolling," I stated the obvious. He said six simple saving words: "Take your foot off the clutch." He was right. In my angst to restart that truck, my leg was still pressing down as hard as it possibly could on the clutch, and when I removed it, I immediately stopped my descent.

My rescuing farmer jumped out of his truck and quickly assessed the situation. That ripped key was unusable, so I was going nowhere (although he applauded my superhuman strength!). He found some sturdy rocks in the ditch to place behind my wheels. After ascertaining that my dad was indeed on his way and I'd be safe, he carried on to the elevator where he no doubt had a story to tell those gathered around the coffee pot about a girl who didn't know much about a split-shift transmission and a heavy load on a truck.

My dad had the graciousness, even after that incident, to tell me often that I'd make a good farmer someday. It wasn't to be, but it also wasn't the end of heavy loads parked precariously on the steep hill of life.

A schoolhouse is full of such stories. Some were easy to see. It was the young family who watched disease waste away their father, face the grief of his passing, and the stark reality of their being left almost destitute. Their breadwinner was gone, leaving them with few viable options in a bleak world. It was the teenager who every day gathered her young siblings after school and herded them out the door, struggling under the unwanted responsibility she bore until her single parent came home. It was the preschooler who arrived to pick up his sister, consistently wearing a long wig and dress, his body and mind already questioning what would become a long discovery of identity and finding a comfortable place in his own body. And it was the six-year-old who came to us from a school where expectations were so high and stringent (even in Kindergarten) that the tension kept her body rigid with fear in her desk until unworldly howls erupted into our hallways, like a terrifying nightmare escaping from her throat. What a long hill with a heavy load these youngsters were climbing so early in their innocent lives.

Often, we don't know about the loads others carry even though they have spent many years with us. They walk daily among us without alerting us to the struggle.

It was a classmate's sleepover that alerted us to hardship. Partially to attend our school and meet tuition costs, and partially due to a bad economy, four children slept each night on foam mattresses on the floor in the cramped rooms of a small home.

It wasn't until months and months of trying to stop and redirect a Junior High's hostile and aggressive behaviour that we realized he was at the brunt of hostile and aggressive patterns at home.

And when a ten-year-old arrived at the Christmas concert carrying a knife, we found so many troubled, disturbing layers beneath that incident that only serious intervention would move him forward.

The prophet Isaiah exhorts the people of Judah to *"learn to do good; seek justice, rescue the oppressed, defend the orphan, plead for the widow"*

> We are CALLED to jump into it—to learn, SEEK, rescue, defend, PLEAD.

(Isaiah 1:17). These are active verbs that don't allow us to sit back and observe life from the sideline. We are called to jump into it—to learn, seek, rescue, defend, plead. Each of these verbs is done concerning someone else. We are admonished to earnestly become an advocate to the troubled within our communities and beyond. And, there will come a time when we need that helping hand, that wise word, that act of compassion.

At times, that advocacy is a long journey. At other times, we briefly become part of someone's life. The length of time doesn't correspond to the impact. We can have short encounters that change lives. Certainly, a farmer coming alongside me for a few minutes may have saved me from tipping into the ditch, but perhaps he saved me from a more threatening danger—crashing with severe consequences at the bottom of a hill. His wise and calm six words averted catastrophe.

I recall a clear image of one of our international students sitting in the atrium, bent over a smattering of textbooks. Immersed in a short story he was trying to understand, he transcribed every single word, page after page, scribbling above the tiny space above each sentence a translation into his native language. It was hugely painstaking. Before he could absorb theme, literary nuance, or language expression, he had to figure out what it said. His work was at least double that of his fellow native-speaking classmates. In a science textbook, he wasn't just figuring out the translation. He was trying to absorb complex theories and relevant experiments—a daunting task in one's native tongue. It was many times more difficult as a second language.

I remember sitting with him for an hour and explaining the scientific concepts under study. It was hard work. Occasionally, he would catch a glimmer of what I was saying and nod, giving me a big smile to show that he was with me and we could move on. It was a brief window of endless hours of study he had each day to reach the goal of living in a different land and finding a new life. His determination was inspiring. His profuse thanks for the little ways we helped him along was undeserved. Yet, I was most keenly aware that when I returned to my office and my work, I was leaving him to carry that burden alone. He did this day after day, week after week, buried under the unrelenting avalanche of assignments in every subject. I wonder now if I did enough. Did I provide him with words and actions that inspired him to carry on? I hope I helped place a stone behind the wheels to stop him rolling to disaster, to still his fearful heart when the engine to get up that long hill was sputtering.

So keep an eye out. Someone is waiting for you to roll up beside them and help them along the way. Paul instructs us to *"bear one another's burdens and in this way you will fulfill the law of Christ"* (Galatians 6:2). It is an instruction to take to heart to help those in our community make it through life's complexities. After recess one day, one of our young students said to the supervising teacher: "You'd better take my hand while I go down the stairs. Sometimes I can't control what happens." Exactly. Hold out your hand, someone is out of control, and you are the person to help.

CHAPTER 17
GLIMPSES OF ETERNITY

For now we see in a mirror, dimly, but then we will see face to face. Now I know only in part; then I will know fully, even as I have been fully known. (1 Corinthians 13:12)

For a moment, I stood quietly at the classroom door to still my heart and watched her. She was nine. Her dark hair flowed down her back, and she had that chiselled look of an Egyptian queen with the regal name to match, Maura. She was laughing at something her classmate said while at the same time madly erasing scribbles on her paper. There would be no erasing what I was about to tell her. Her parents had called from their doctor's office and needed to bring her in to assess a fast-growing tumour. They wanted to tell Maura with me present in my office. There was an uncontrollable hitch in their voice. Would I go get her? And here I was standing at the precipice, unable to pull her into the divide. I was about to take her from this carefree moment and relay words that could change her life. I wanted to give her a few more minutes to be untouched by this.

Maura came happily when I called and took my hand. She chattered as we climbed the stairs to my office, telling me about what she was learning. I smiled back, but my brain was tumbling with the possibilities of this moment. If she was startled to see her parents in my office, she didn't show it. She plopped into a chair and looked at us expectantly. I then recognized that it was me who would be learning the most important lesson that day.

For some kids, our time together isn't about learning for their future. Their learning and living are only now, and their precious time isn't measured in years. The tendency is to look long term. We want our kids to become productive, caring citizens; we want to give them the tools to lead a responsible life. But we do so at the expense of the opportunity for here and now.

Today, these children are given the opportunity to laugh, love, and cry. Today, these children are here for us to affirm and challenge. These children are actively involved in the process of living—they are being educated for life that is only certain for this moment. A teacher may not expect this divine perspective to emerge. In those idealistic days of first entering a classroom, teachers aren't prepared to encounter moments when we don't look forward but rather upward to glimpse eternity. Even with the very young.

As difficult as it was, our little group didn't rush through the moment. We sat together in that sunny, sacred space, tears brimming and hearts unsteady. The words of Maura's parents tumbled out—there would be a test, it would give important information and then a plan would be put in place to deal with the growth. I watched those big brown eyes try to absorb those adult words, to process as much as a child possibly could. Maura gave a tentative nod. And when they all turned to me and asked me to pray, we held hands, and I said the only words I could, "Stay near to us, dear Jesus."

"Stay NEAR to US, dear JESUS."

"Stay near to us, dear Jesus" became words that grounded me when further heart-wrenching situations crept into my world. What more can we ask for? In a world where each of us climbs mountaintops and steps unwittingly into the deepest of valleys, we need our Saviour to stay near.

It was one such day when I was standing in a windy cemetery with childhood friends as we clustered around the too-early grave of our friend. For reasons we would never know, his motorcycle careened over an embankment on a winding mountain road. Although the wind was whipping around our clothes and hair as we lingered near this final resting place, the poignant words of the priest pierced into my heart. "I believe in a God who weeps at the roadside of an accident." What? Could it be that the divine also weeps for us? How that comforted me!

That the Master, the Lord of all, shared our pain and sadness became bedrock to my faith. In what was a tangle of metal and debris on a mountain road, there stood our Saviour weeping. We know he wept at Lazarus's grave. And if we skip randomly forward in the gospel of John, when Mary Magdalene stood weeping in grief at the holy One's tomb, she didn't recognize the Lord until he said her name. "Mary." And she said one word back: "Teacher." I have imagined that scene over and over. There were no long words to explain the resurrection. Just her name. And his. The most beautiful of combinations! It is the most poignant verse in the entire Bible because someday, there will be a time when we hear our name, and it will be the Lord. He weeps for us. He calls us by name.

So, when sometime later an accident, on a rare, snowy day in early October, claimed the mother of two of our students, I knew that I had words to share: That our Lord was also on that icy road. That he wept with us. That her name was on his lips. When the length of life is suddenly halted, when we are forced to look at our finite being and see the pain of those who hurt around us, we recognize again that we don't weep alone. There is One who stands beside us and then he looks to his people to act.

I love the words of Teresa of Ávila:

> Christ has no body now but yours. No hands, no feet on earth but yours.
> Yours are the eyes through which he looks compassion on this world.
> Yours are the feet with which he walks to do good.
> Yours are the hands through which he blesses all the world.
> Yours are the hands, yours are the feet, yours are the eyes, you are his body.
> Christ has no body now on earth but yours.[7]

---

[7] St. Teresa of Ávila (attributed). https://catholic-link.org/quotes/st-teresa-of-avila-quote-christ-has-no-body-but-yours/

This is our task in God's world. We need to shine God's love in deliberate ways, whether in the tragic situations of life or the ordinary moments of the day. Our children need to experience God's love through us, modelled in our relationships and our care for each other. And as we parent and teach, with patience, prayer, love, and laughter, our children will be learning the most valuable life lesson of all.

The Psalms also assure us that we are not alone. God watches over us. "*The Lord is your keeper; the Lord is your shade at your right hand.... The Lord will keep your going out and your coming in from this time on and for-evermore*" (Psalm 121:5,8). This was beautifully illustrated on a sweltering Saturday as I sat with a group of people watching an outdoor passion play. There was something comforting and reassuring in hearing the stories of Jesus's life and ministry again. What captivated my imagination, and the young children around me, were the angels who appeared and reappeared unexpectedly and randomly throughout the play. The hills that naturally created the set hosted sporadic and unexpected sightings of celestial beings. They came and went silently. During the final scene, the cast and audience were surrounded completely by a company of angels, including the risen Lord. It was a striking visual reminder of the constant presence of God's angels in the lives of his people. One week later, when a horse fatally kicked a seven year old boy from our group, it became even more relevant. That compelling image of the angels watching and surrounding us became one of comfort for the family and friends of this little boy, who had now joined that company of angels.

The more I thought about this boy and the purpose of his short life, the more I kept returning to the story of the child Samuel who God persistently and lovingly called when the *"word of the Lord was rare"*(1 Samuel 3:1). It strikes me that, in a time of spiritual darkness, God called one of the youngest in his flock. God placed that child where he could be mentored and established throughout Israel as a prophet. Why should we expect anything less? While we prepare our students for the future, their lives are being lived here and now. God is speaking to the boys and girls among us. He has given us the opportunity and challenge of raising these children and young people towards the growth of his kingdom. But he is also using them in their present lives.

When a new family joined our school they came from a place without a faith background. As their young girl heard Bible stories at school, she brought them home to the dinner table. Wanting to stay abreast of what their child was learning, the mother came to my office one day with a Bible in hand and said, "Could I ask you some questions?" How my heart quickened; something holy was going on here! It was a small and giant step from those seeking conversations to this family joining with a local congregation that embraced them into their fold. When a life-threatening illness weakened the mother's body, that congregation stayed close. And when eternity opened up for her, she stepped right in as a child redeemed. God said her name. God's hand was in that story all along in a mighty way. It began with an innocent faith of a young girl in our school and blossomed with eternal consequences for the entire family.

And so, we stumble on. Each day brings us closer to our last. For Maura, there was a reprieve as with gratitude we learned that her tumour was benign. For her, further education, a career, motherhood, and a full life still beckoned and were realized. But the lesson from that day still echoes in my soul: Stay near us dear Jesus, even into the arms of eternity.

CHAPTER 18

THE STRENGTH OF COMMUNITY

*The gatekeeper opens the gate for him, and the sheep hear
his voice. He calls his own sheep by name and leads them
out.* (John 10:3)

For at least a year, I had a trainee on my morning rounds opening
the school. She was about six, and she would seek me out at 7:30
each morning just as the early morning sun rays were spilling into our
many windows. She would grab one end of my lanyard with the school
keys, and I would hold the other end. With this cord between us, we
started on our way. Together, we opened a multitude of locks in common rooms and stairwells. Strangely, the locks weren't uniform, and it
took some figuring to determine how each one opened. I felt a bit like
a parent handing over car keys when we switched to her opening the
doors instead of me. She always had a look of dogged determination as
she mumbled, "Now, which way does this one turn?" before she heard
a satisfying click. It was a bit disconcerting when she started pointing
out maintenance issues before me, but it tickled me that she was gaining
a new perspective on school life beyond her classroom; she was already
learning about doing her part for the community she was a part of.

Each day, this opening of the school with one of the youngest
and oldest members became a symbolic preparation for those in our
community who would enter the doors a short time later. A community
at its best gives equal value to each member. While their roles are
different, their importance is the same.

A little girl poked her head in my office one day, holding up
dripping boots and said, "I'm just going to put these boots on your rug

to dry off." I hid my happy smile as she, without ceremony, plunked them down and scuttled off. Well, why not? My room is your room. A teacher has nothing to teach without her students. A sports team needs a coach to hold it together and provide strategic direction. No youngster skates at lunch unless a bunch of volunteers first put down their heads to lace up skates. We provide a symbolic key to others' lives when we welcome the stranger or create a sense of belonging to a shared cause.

For decades, being a good school for a bunch of kids was only part of our mandate. Surviving was the other part. And that part was hard. Financial realities resulted in many late-night board meetings figuring out how to make it another month, another year. Buildings we were renting were suddenly unavailable, and we had the daunting task of having to quickly find a new home and move an entire school community time after time. There was no way to get through those obstacles without a dedicated community. Families sold their homes to move into a neighbourhood close to the school, or else they made long commutes across the city. Every year, on top of tuition and government grants, the community raised piles of money to stay afloat. There were live auctions and silent auctions and skate-a-thons and chocolate sales. Parents, grandparents, and past families made sacrifices of time and money. Teachers took pay cuts and would forgo a pension. But it was perhaps in that desperate bid to keep something we so believed in alive that we grew our most important resource—a community—dedicated to raising the children God had given us.

It's always been a point of curiosity that Jesus didn't tell parables about his trade. In the gospels, you don't find a parable that starts, "A carpenter picked up his hammer...." Instead, Jesus tells story after story about sheep and the shepherd. He talks about the intimacy of a shepherd who calls the sheep by name (John 10:3), about his identity as the good shepherd who lays down his life for his sheep (John 10:11), about the persistence of a shepherd leaving the flock to hunt down one, lost sheep (Luke 15), and even about the inevitable separation of the goats and the sheep (Matthew 25:32). Jesus consistently builds on this literary imagery: a lost, misguided, stubbornly endearing flock and the compassionate shepherd trying to keep the flock together. Our communities, like that flock of sheep, require care and love for each member to reach the larger, shared purpose of kingdom building.

We had a bit of excitement at school one wintry day. An older woman in the neighbourhood became dizzy, fell on the sidewalk alongside our school, and hit her head. When she tried to get up, she started weaving toward the road. A woman driving by stopped, got out and helped her to our school. Several of us ran out, placed the woman on cushions, covered her with jackets, and called 911. Our compassionate office volunteer knelt beside our lady, held her hand, and kept talking to her to keep her alert. As circumstances would have it, it was the beginning of our school noon hour, and our kids were milling about in the sunshine, ready to cross to the playground. Into this ordered chaos, drove the ambulance. While we waited for the paramedics, we ushered worried students across to the playground.

About that time, I looked up to our glass doors, and there stood a cross-grade section of students, crowding around the window, watching. I walked up the stairs to talk to them, and the first question I heard was, "Is she going to be okay?" *Genuine concern.* The next statement surprised me, although it shouldn't have.

A group of our Junior High boys, who had at points challenged us with their exuberance and energy, looked intently at me and said, "If she slipped on some ice, we better make sure there is no ice or snow on any of our stairs or sidewalk. Could we take some shovels out this lunch hour and make sure everything is cleared off?" *Great forward-looking plan.*

When I returned from my afternoon class to the office, there was our same office volunteer on the phone, making sure our lady had made it home okay and inquiring about her health. She called her every hour until her family was able to be with her. She even arranged for flowers to be delivered to her home. *Compassionate follow up.*

I think the best lesson that day was the community cohesion to rally behind a stranger who was hurt. It was the understanding that many can contribute to the needs of one and that the efforts of many contribute to the building of the kingdom. It was a scene I would repeatedly see on small and large scales in our community. I loved recess times. Students across grades would organize a mass soccer game quickly and seamlessly, and the best of individual students often shone through. It was older students graciously letting younger students join their fast-paced game, letting it slow down when the ball haphazardly grazed into the periphery of the young and inexperienced. It was an older student who picked up a fallen youngster in the fray of things, and with a pat on the head, pushed them back in the game. It was the utter admiration of a young boy watching his older buddy break through the crowd and maneuver until he had a great shot on the net and cheered him on wildly. It was three Grade one girls who were allowed to stand completely in the way even though they contributed nothing other than a giggle and an excited exuberance for being in the moment. It gave me great satisfaction as a teacher to watch this unfold without adult intervention. It showed potential for what might come when it wasn't a soccer game anymore. It was a glimpse into the best of community living.

In chapel one morning, our oldest students demonstrated how weak a single strand of string was. It broke apart easily with a pull. They kept adding more strands, weaving them together, then gave the same push and pull. The strands became a rope that became stronger, sturdier, and unbreakable. So we, too, can we make it through the scrapes of life. Jesus banded an unlikely and weak menagerie of followers together to become his disciples. They would go on with strength and vision to build the world-changing early church. We hear and recognize that same voice and heed the call of the shepherd to follow him. At our best, we are a community that, through genuine concern, a forward-looking plan, and compassionate follow-up, cares for the stranger among us. We open locks to invite others into the flock of the Great Shepherd, who calls us each by name.

CHAPTER 19
THE UNEXPECTED PATH

In all your ways acknowledge him, and he will make straight your paths. (Proverbs 3:6)

There was a break between the final session at the Administrators' Retreat, held at a mountain lodge. So, together with a couple of friends, we decided to squeeze in a walk in our beautiful setting. I was regaling the group with a story our students had heard in chapel recently. The speaker had been lost in this very same area.

His rescue story was dramatic and kept our students spellbound. We considered that as we kept walking, leaving the main path into forest and brush, following a variety of little animal paths that veered closer to the river. Eventually, we had walked all the way down from the lodge to the golf course—a considerable distance down a steep valley. We gazed at the river and walked along beside it, following an increasingly dwindling path. When we started parting the branches ahead of us, I had my first clue that we had lost any sense of pathway. Going back was an option, but we had come a fair distance. Now we were about forty-five minutes away from losing daylight, and we needed the quickest option back before darkness descended. What to do? We decided to go straight up, through trees and brush, past trampled grass where animals obviously had been resting, and even past some large bones that had been a carnivore's lunch.

After scaling the first ravine, we recognized that we weren't reaching the pathway, so we went all the way down another ravine and up again. Again, we weren't as close as we thought we'd be, so we headed down our third ravine and climbed up. We constantly looked for the ridge and where the sun was so that we would keep our perspective. Suddenly, the lost hiker story from chapel seemed too ironic for comfort! After the third ravine, we were trying to gain our perspective in the trees and were considering a deer path to walk along. I turned my head and stared through the trees, where I saw an individual walking briskly about a hundred metres away. "Well," I said, "we could follow the deer path, or we could just join the paved path!" We were found.

Life is like that. We're stumbling along, not always paying complete attention, and suddenly we've journeyed to an area that's not entirely comfortable. There are obstacles at every turn, and it's disconcerting that you can't see the end in sight. But the combination of friends along the journey to toss ideas back and forth, commiserate over the experience, and a constant gaze upward to the One who anchors our perspective helps us navigate the way. A journey that, although at points anxious and difficult, was significant in its own way.

When we moved into our new school, the pattern of the tiles on our atrium floor provided all sorts of fun for our younger students. The Grade twos were the first to discover them in September. The coloured tiles, it seemed to them, weren't meant to be walked on normally, but instead to be jumped on, from colour to colour like hopscotch, until a destination was reached or an adult moved them along. From their perspective, there were many pathways, and each one was an adventure. Once I watched a three-year-old, alone in the atrium, leap from tile to tile, occupying herself for a long time as she took little journeys in our sunny room. I wish I'd had a printout of what was going on in her brain. Despite our deliberate planning and designing, this unplanned pathway brought innocent joy.

The book of Ruth tells of an unexpected pathway brought about by harsh circumstances. There is no sugarcoating the scenario in which Naomi and her daughters-in-law, Orpah and Ruth, found themselves. It wasn't a path of their choosing.

All three had lost their husbands, and Naomi's raw assessment was that *"the Almighty has dealt bitterly with me"* (Ruth 1:20). Naomi and her daughters-in-law started the journey back to Naomi's home in Judah. Along the way, with Naomi's pleading, Orpah decided to return to her people. Ruth, however, was unmoved by the logic of this plea and stayed loyal to her mother-in-law. Together Naomi and Ruth took the path back to Judah. Through this unexpected pathway, the pieces of the pattern began to fall into place: Ruth met Boaz, and they married and had a son named Obed. Naomi's friends tell her this grandson shall be the *"restorer of life"* (Ruth 4:15). And he was, not just for a woman in her waning years and a daughter-in-law who was faithful to her, but to a seed that would foster the lineage of Jesse and David—and eventually Jesus, the Saviour of the world.

The story of Ruth not only hints that God's blessings may come from following an unknown path, it also pushes us to consider who is along the journey with us. Ruth had a parental family to return to in Moab, but she chose to stay with a widow, seemingly alone in the world. It was a compassionate decision. It was also life-changing.

Expanding our students' worldview was always on the top of our minds—to inspire them to follow Ruth's example: choose a compassionate pathway that considers others. We hoped it would be life-changing. Around Halloween, we hosted a Penny Carnival for our students. It was a lively event with booths throughout the gym where they could throw beanbags, have a pillow fight, get their faces painted, and all manner of creative activities. With each loonie they put down, there was a purpose: to help students in the Ukraine whose school environment was far less advantageous than ours.

From my vantage point as a ticket-taker, I surveyed the organized chaos. One of our oldest students caught my eye. He was hanging around the edges, watching events unfold but wasn't joining in. Occasionally he bantered with his peers, but he didn't come by to purchase tickets so he could partake. I couldn't quite figure out what was going on as he was usually in the thick of things.

At the end of the afternoon, I told the students that I would stand by the gym doors as they exited. If they wanted to make a further donation of their excess loonies on their way out they could place it in a tin I was holding. There was no pressure—it was just an offered opportunity. The youth who'd been at the edges came close to me and pulled out his wallet. I watched in amazement as he emptied the entire thing—bills and coins from his allowance and lawn mowing came tumbling out and landed without a word in my tin. He gave everything he had, singlehandedly increasing our donation amount significantly. And he would have kept walking if I hadn't grabbed his arm to thank him. While circling the gym, he had been thinking about people in a world across the ocean. He was moved by compassion and care not to hold back one bit. In his usual quiet way, he said, "It's for those kids."

> Our pathways are not just a ROUTE to our destination but an OPPORTUNITY to encounter another, known or UNKNOWN.

I am humbled that I can learn from a silent, teenage benefactor about the infinite goodness of God's grace, gratitude, and giving. I also need to learn that wherever I am on life's pathway, I need to consider who is on the journey with me. What has happened in our busy, productive worlds that has taken our sight away from others? Our pathways are not just a route to our destination but an opportunity to encounter another, known or unknown. God help us when we step over them in pursuit of our noble causes.

I think back to that three-year-old navigating the pattern of tiles in our atrium. She was playing in a safe spot, plotting an imaginative journey in her mind. I imagine where her life might take her in the future, on a bunch of hopscotch journeys. Some pathways will be easy, inspiring, and fulfilling. She will revel in them, solid foundations of the paved path of life, and the glory of the view. There will be other pathways not of her choosing. They may be illness, tragedy, betrayal, heartbreak, and grief. She may spiral down these pathways and keep taking little exits that take her farther and farther away from what she knows to be the right direction. But there is a way back, even if it is often difficult and obscured. There will be people close by and in far corners of the world whose lives she could touch. I hope she has the compassion to stop and help. And most of all, I hope she keeps her eyes on the horizon, always looking up. If she does, that beautiful reflection of sunlight through the clouds, a light that shines on the tile she skips onto even now, will find her and will not leave. It's a glimpse of the glory and the gaze of the One who won't take his eye off her until the end of her days.

CHAPTER 20
DUST

All go to the same place; all come from dust, and to dust all return. (Ecclesiastes 3:20)

Dust. It gathered surreptitiously in the corners of classrooms and bathrooms because the caretaker's broom was wide and unwieldly, and the corners were sharp, accurate, and refined. It swirled harshly out of the sandpit the long jumpers leapt into, forcing them to shield their eyes and turn away from the sting. It gathered on the base of boot racks, the forgotten debris of a day's hard play in mud puddles sent to earth to delight the young.

Dust. It was in the ductwork of our brand-new school. Drywall dust lazily floated and dipped silently in the HVAC pipes. It was the September long weekend, and we were madly moving an entire school into our new building before school started on Tuesday. It was exhilarating and exhausting. And now, close to sunset, only a handful of us were left. I was mopping the atrium floor, readying it for our students who would sit on it for the first hour of the first day. It was holy work, erasing dusty footprints and preparing a clean floor for those who would carry their souls into our school and start this new chapter. My bones were weary, but I was determined it would glisten for day one—a clean slate, a new promised land.

A voice from upstairs carried down with more energy than the late hour allowed. "I smell smoke." Heads lifted from mops and boxes, and drills lifted mid-air, poised to install a bulletin board. As one we inhaled, and it was true, something was hot, maybe burning, although there was no flame visible. Someone had the presence of mind to summon all the stragglers from the far corners of the school and shoo us outside to stand in a cluster on the front steps. We called 911 and waited the interminable minutes for fire trucks to arrive. "We need to pray," another said, and we clustered even tighter together, heads bowed, hands on each other's shoulders, and a plea was sent heavenward.

Except for me. I was glad to be among such hallowed friends, but prayer wasn't in me. My words were more like incredulity flung skyward. It was all I could do to breathe past the lump in my throat, the tears leaking unbidden from my eyes. While the rest bowed, I stared at the school, encased in that group from where I stood. I stared and stared, waiting for flames to appear. I couldn't blink. Surely not, Lord. Surely you haven't brought us this close after so long of a journey only to burn down a school before even one student crossed the threshold.

The distant sirens wailed and turned into our driveway, pointing out the first flaw of our new build. The large vehicle scraped against the incline of the drive, causing the first scars but not the last. As the firefighters' examination discovered, the drywall dust in the vents was indeed what we were detecting. While it needed to be looked after, our building wasn't in danger. We exhaled breaths we didn't know we were holding.

If a mote of dust can cause a spark, I wonder what that says about our souls. If it is indeed true, as C.S. Lewis writes, that we are all souls who happen to have bodies, is the soul represented by a spark that began with dust? Ecclesiastes tells us, "from dust we came and from dust we return." It seems that there is so much potential, and so much that is sacred, in the lowly dab of dust.

I was rushing home from school one night to be in time for trick or treaters. I was just hanging up my coat and shedding the debris of the day when the doorbell first chimed. Opening the door revealed delight. There stood a mother dressed in an elaborate ladybug costume, holding a baby—maybe seven months—in an identical ladybug costume. I smiled, greeting them, and was about to reach for a chocolate bar to hand out when the baby extended her arms and leaned purposefully toward me. "Is it okay?" I asked the mom as I gathered the baby into my arms. She seemed baffled by her baby's initiative. "She won't ever go to anyone other than me," she marvelled. But for some reason, here was innocence personified, cradled in my arms, and I positioned her so that we could look at each other. You know the phrase *soulful gaze*? That's what happened. That baby locked eyes with me and wouldn't look away. It didn't feel like I was looking at a baby, but a spark of her soul, fizzing on a wire and connecting with mine. Age was meaningless. It was with reluctance, and no small amount of awe, that I handed that beautiful ladybug back.

This encounter changed my thinking, and I started to wonder what it would be like to see someone's soul rather than their body. What if we could look past the limp, tattered outer shell, the spit and polish? I started looking deliberately for everyone's soul, their light that had been sparked by dust. It is the way our Saviour sees us—a shimmering soul encased by the body—that helps us do the work we are sent to do. It made a difference in my perspective, whether in a seniors' lodge, my back office, or a church lobby when I tried to see past the outer shell.

I pondered this truth as I sat silently on a boat with a friend, bobbing on the water with the motor cut, the sun reflected in such a way that the water was inundated with sparkling lights all around us, tipping off each gentle wave. It was as if everyone we had loved that had gone beyond was settling on the water, joining in on the beauty of the moment. Seeing intuitively what I was seeing, my friend remarked, "It's quite something, isn't it?" Quite something indeed. Something sacred.

In one of our first school locations, there was a park nearby. In September, my young Grade ones could be overwhelmed by the length of the day, and occasionally we would stop and take a short trip to the park to clear our brains and stretch our legs. My student with muscular dystrophy had only so much physical capability, so sometimes, I ended up piggybacking him on the return trip. He was a solid weight hanging onto my shoulders; unable to grip with his legs, and sometimes those last steps were heavy ones. Now I see it differently. It wasn't an able body carrying an injured body. It was a vibrant soul, carried by another, each brilliant and shimmering. Bodies were burdened. The souls were not.

When pandemic restrictions finally eased, I was able to visit a church I hadn't been in for over a year. As I was exiting the service, a masked lady, bent over a walker, grabbed my hand. It took me a bit to recognize her. The mask obscured her face, but it was something else that had changed her: it was grief, shrouding her like a heavy blanket. The first words I said were, "You've had a hard year." She nodded and told me that in a short, seven-month period, she had lost her son to cancer. Because of restrictions, they had just now been able to have a funeral. With a walker awkwardly between us, I put my arm around her, and again I felt the connection—not of a frail, bent body—her soul connected to mine, immediately joined despite a long absence. In a final gesture, as much a groan as a sigh of resignation, she placed her head close to my shoulder and whispered, "It was God's will." Perhaps there is nothing more to say other than our souls connect around the will of God. To have been placed for much of my career in a school built for this purpose was a divine gift.

> Perhaps there is nothing MORE to say other than our SOULS CONNECT around the will of GOD.

Dust. At rest in a school corner. Swirling hidden in a pipe. Dormant on a boot rack. Flickering to life in the womb. From dust, we come. And from dust, we will return. But in some miraculous way, the dust of a carbon atom becomes a diamond. The dust of our lives becomes a soul, shining and reflecting the light of God.

Dust.

A spark.

CHAPTER 21
LOVE AND A PLAYDOUGH COOKIE

I have loved you with an everlasting love; therefore I have continued my faithfulness to you. (Jeremiah 31:3, ESV)

It was the end of the day after a long week. When I'd seen my Grade one class list earlier in August, I was amused but not worried. There were only two girls on the list. Yes, two. And a whole bunch of boys. It was just about what you'd expect: a bit wild and a bit wonderful all at the same time. It was the year of "eau de cologne little boy." Quite stinky. And when the class clown fell dramatically from his chair, maybe accidentally on purpose, he, of course, had to accidentally on purpose repeat that three times because it got such a great reaction.

We were nearing the point of four falls from the chair, severely waning attention, and a clock that was close to school dismissal but not quite freeing us all into the weekend. Late afternoon sun rays were barely lighting up the classroom. I sighed and gave up on the science lesson that was no longer riveting—maybe never was—and made a deal. We would ditch science, and they could have twenty minutes of free time at blocks, puzzles, games, playdough, or books with one condition: I was able to mark their math books and not be disturbed. They jumped at the opportunity and were soon engaged in their respective choices, energy still abounding. I sunk wearily into my chair, energy not abounding, and for a full minute contemplated putting my head on the lopsided pile of math books teetering on my desk. Regretfully, I picked up my marking pen and started on the pile.

Of course, it wasn't long before I sensed a shadow at my elbow. What did I expect? They were six; they weren't going to manage on their own. Even so, I shook my head and kept marking. The shadow stayed. Exasperated, I turned my head and said, "Remember, do not disturb. That's our deal." Staring back at me was a freckled face with a sheepish grin. He was looking at me expectantly. Both his hands were cupped around something, and he offered it to me without a word. When he opened his hands, I felt such remorse and dismay. It was like a needle stabbed into my side. Sticking to dirty hands was a playdough cookie, and inscribed with some sharp tool were the words, *I love you.* Oh, stinky little boy, you are the teacher today. I opened my arms.

When we are on a collective journey, our time together isn't without stumbles. It took a six-year-old to remind me that while my patience waned too soon, he still offered love. He wasn't put off by my flaws and reminded me to reach with compassion unconditionally to those in my care. It's a characteristic that he emulates from the story of David.

David's story tends to leap between high mountain peaks and low valleys. His strength of character was abundantly evident. He was anointed by Samuel as God's chosen, bravely refuting the use of armour as he slew Goliath, fierce as a warrior in battle, gentle and melodic as a musician and songwriter, a loyal friend to Jonathan, and a tender provider to Jonathan's son Mephibosheth. David had so much good.

And yet, David missed the mark equally dramatically. His conquests weren't just on the battlefield. On the rooftop, he seduced Bathsheba, who conceived his child; David then intricately and savagely plotted the death of her husband Uriah to cover his sin. The Lord sent the prophet Nathan to show David his displeasure. Despite all that David had been given—king over Israel, rescued from Saul, given the house of Israel and Judah (2 Samuel 12:7–9)—he did evil in the sight of the Lord. There was so much destruction.

And the consequences pile up for David as the Lord said he would *"raise up trouble... from within [David's] own house"* (2 Samuel 12:11). Devastatingly, the life of the child born by Bathsheba was taken. Sorrow upon sorrow. Yet, when David went to comfort Bathsheba after their son's death, and Solomon was born as a result, what are the Lord's words regarding this new birth? *"The Lord loved him"* (2 Samuel 12:24). The words weren't inscribed on a playdough cookie, but they were delivered by the prophet Nathan. It's kind of the same. It's a faithful, enduring love that trickled down unbidden from generation to generation.

None of our lives echo in broad strokes the dramatic swings of David's life. But in smaller brush strokes, they do. We take strong and beautiful steps that bless God's kingdom. But we also stumble devastatingly, and God shows mercy.

A broom closet isn't the best place for a serious conversation, but it was where I found myself with a Junior High girl who pulled me in as she needed privacy for her confession. She was trying to extract a promise that I wouldn't tell her parents what she was about to reveal, a promise I couldn't make. The words tumbled out of her anyway. Her boyfriend from another school was showing up at her house late at night, convincing her to sneak out. She was conflicted. Sneaking out and the attention of an older boy was more than a bit exhilarating. It was also risky. It would get her in trouble, whatever that nebulous word meant. Yet, of course, with teenage hormones surging, they were exploring that winding pathway of making their own decisions that inevitably had consequences.

It was tricky getting involved in scenarios that didn't happen on school grounds. It wasn't my purview, but the safety of students was. With the mops and dustpans listening, we talked over her options, although she mainly shook her head vigorously at me as all of them involved talking with her parents. I finally agreed to a twenty-four-hour window where she could try to resolve the situation on her own terms and then have a hard conversation with her parents. I didn't need to be directly involved, but knowing what I did, it may come to that if she failed to follow through. She agreed not to leave her house under cover of darkness that night and to have the needed conversation with her boyfriend on the phone regarding boundaries. I told her I would keep my cell phone on if she felt coerced, but I was also keeping her parents' number beside me. I wanted to give her the opportunity to start trying on adult shoes, yet I needed to be the safety net if she couldn't.

What were the right words for parents to say in this situation? They did it correctly with: *We love you. You're grounded.* Both statements meant the same thing. This turn of events resulted in a strain on my relationship with her. In confiding in me, it wasn't her hope or intent to get grounded. There were no more broom-closet meetings, and she avoided me until we found our way again with the passage of time, the slow creep back into the ordinariness of a school day.

Our story came full circle many years later when she sent me pictures of her young children. I chuckled at the thought that they might also be sneaking out in a few years, and then she would be in a different position! But there was also a sense of peace in how the world tilts when we stumble but also offers us an opportunity to show compassion and turn things right.

I feel comfort in the tender expression of God's love. It is everlasting and eternal. It is offered freely, graciously, and innocently as words of love etched on a playdough cookie. It survives the inevitable tough falls from grace we each experience. It is new every morning. It is God himself, creator of the universe, watch-keeper of our every step lest we stumble or fall. For God is love.

CHAPTER 22
LAYER UPON LAYER

It is the Lord who goes before you. He will be with you; he will not fail you or forsake you. Do not fear or be dismayed. (Deuteronomy 31:8)

We called the basketball play *Race*. When facing tight pressure on the sidelines or a full-court press, my girls would yell *Race,* and everyone sprang into action. The guards standing just near the sideline stood back-to-back to receive the ball. Our tallest forward held the basketball aloft on the sideline while the other players stayed out of the key. The guards locked pinkies while the opposition stood confused at this bizarre arrangement, unsure how to defend. On the silent signal of a squeezed pinkie, the guards spun on their inside shoulders, racing in opposite directions, ensuring that at least one of them was usually free in the confusion. From there, it was a quick lob-pass to the open guard, a further pass to the centre, who was now running into the key, and if all went as planned, an easy two points. We didn't need to dribble the ball once.

From my place on the bench, I held my breath as *Race* was set up in the final minute of our game. We were so close to winning the tournament. We were the smallest school and had been invited at the last minute. A bigger school pulled out, so to round out the roster, they asked us to join. There was an understanding from the tournament organizer that as a small school, we would have to bring our Grade nine players along as well to a Grade seven and eight tournament. Even so, our bench was short. And there was zero expectation from our host school that we would be in a winning position at any time.

But here we were in the finals! The pinkie squeeze was given, the play went into motion, and the basket swished as the buzzer sounded. The girls gathered in a group hug. It had been a display of grit, speed, and a sneaky little play. We won.

"Be good sports," I admonished the girls. "Shake hands; thank the opposition for a good game, and then line up for your trophy." They did as asked, and I watched them line up at centre court, sweaty and pleased with themselves for a scrappy win. They waited while the organizers huddled. It became awkward when people started leaving the gym. Even the refs packed up. When the girls gave me an inquiring look, I just shrugged my shoulders. Not understanding the delay any more than them, I called them in to sit with me.

Finally, a grim tournament organizer pulled me aside. "We're not giving you the trophy," he informed me. "Your Grade nine players disqualify you. We'll have a different trophy made up for you instead."

It was a quiet ride home, a subdued and hollow victory.

In the grand scheme of things, this was a small problem. I sometimes wonder how different life would be if called to something adventurous like the mission field or a surgeon holding life in her hands with the cut of a scalpel. On the other hand, Mother Teresa clarifies for us that "not all of us can do great things. But we can do small things with great love."[8] Teaching is like that. We take the moments that unfold around us, and we use them as a layer. Moment after moment, we work through the lesson presented to us; sometimes, it's in the curriculum, but mostly it's in life. Our fervent prayer is that those layers help shape the character of our students as richly as it shapes ours as we travel the journey together.

> MOMENT after moment, we work through the LESSON presented to us; sometimes, it's in the curriculum, but mostly it's in LIFE.

---

[8] Famously attributed to Mother Teresa.

So, when my girls' team drifted in for practice the next Monday, we didn't go into drills and warm-ups. We sat in a circle and processed what had happened: the thrill of putting together such a good tournament and the disappointment in what felt like an unfair ending. It was beyond our control. We could only control how we responded and how we moved forward with what we learned. We also put it into its proper place as a single moment in a long season. These life lessons were layers I hoped they would apply to other scenarios in their future because it was a pattern I would see repeated in their lives and mine. A single, derailing moment forces us to make a decision—not as to what happens—but how will we respond? As the girls were learning, the strength of your character dictates your response, and you can only influence your response. What others do is out of your hands.

One of the bestselling cakes auctioned off at our Sweet Interlude fundraisers every year was a Napoleon Torte. It wasn't unheard of for it to fetch a four-digit sum. The time-consuming recipe had layer upon layer of cake interspersed with creamy custard. It takes forever to make... and the first bite will tell you it's worth every minute and every penny you forked out (bad pun) at the auction. I think that same culinary patience is what goes into building a life. There is a foundation layer, a creamy layer, a sweet topping. There is the love of a family, the thrill of shared experiences, a multitude of life lessons that require a response, the stark knife wounds we can't control but which provide a lesson.

Layer upon layer, decision upon decision, year after year, we evolve.

I always liked walking by the music rehearsals in our school. It didn't matter whether it was a choir singing, a band figuring out their instruments, a spring musical coming together, or even those squeaky recorders that were about as musical as a crow's caw. There were always several things at play. Notes had to be learned for sure. But equally important, to make music required listening to other musicians, blending a sound, knowing when to contribute and when to pause. Often this resulted in a masterful performance, and sometimes it was the beginning of some musical pursuit that would carry on past the school grounds. It may be as small as a humming student walking out the door with a tune in her heart or as large as a vocation chosen in the musical field. The layers weren't necessarily significant until seen in hindsight as part of the whole.

Not all layers are melodious. Sometimes, the most significant life learnings came from the harshest circumstances, sometimes so dark no shaft of sunlight seemed to break through. I wish that the tough moments our students faced later in life were as mild as being denied a trophy. But they weren't. Stories drifted back to us years after our students left us: severe illness, a drunk driver tragically hitting a vehicle driven by an alumnus and marriages that ended before they had really begun. As teachers, we absorbed these severe life twists from a distance. We had passed these students along; yet we reflected on them with no small amount of sadness and a fervent hope that a foundation had been laid that allowed for courage and strength in adversity.

No story haunted me more, however, than that of Lukas. Lukas was a quiet student with a ready smile. He was kind to others and easy to be around. His time with us was uneventful in a nice kind of way. Lukas was steady and grounded.

Horror struck in 2013 when Lukas was swarmed, beaten, and stabbed outside a Calgary nightclub. He was only eighteen. The events were precipitated by Lukas sticking up for an employee outside the club. Lukas inserted himself in the fray and admonished others that they didn't need to be racist in their comments. It was a testament to his strength of character, to the layers that had been built in him before this moment, that he instinctively reached out with goodness and kindness to one being berated. In a huge injustice, it cost him his life. His kindness was turned against him in the most deadly and brutal way.

It took six long years for Lukas's perpetrators to be brought to justice. It involved a slow progression through the court system and an international manhunt for the suspect who had fled to Vietnam. These were six years where his family was repeatedly drawn back into the nightmare. At long last, a life sentence of twenty-five years with no chance of parole was dispensed for the murderer. This was justice. But it did nothing to alter the day-to-day reality of life without their son.

Most days, I can't process this violent end to a promising young man. I can skim through scripture and not find any meaning or comfort from this senselessness. The only spark I can see is from a family and community that nurtured this boy, that helped him work out, layer by layer, the decisions and situations he faced. Inevitably, it led to this final moment of his graciousness to a stranger. And I have to trust in the words that Moses gave to Joshua in front of Israel as Joshua was going to take over the leadership of Israel.

Moses had helped build the layers of leadership in Joshua's life, including sending him as a spy into the long-awaited Promised Land. But it was Moses's final words to his successor that stand out, urging Joshua to rely on the One who is faithful: *"It is the Lord who goes before you. He will be with you; he will not fail you or forsake you. Do not fear or be dismayed"* (Deuteronomy 31:8).

For our students who are unwittingly walking into scenarios they don't know will come, we can point them to their Comforter, who will not forsake them. And even when evil abounds, as it did that winter night in a downtown alley, I sense an even greater presence did not forsake his child.

Not long after our replacement trophy was finally delivered to our girls' team, a bunch of seven-year-old girls were sent to me to work out recess problems. They were particularly nasty to each other in a way that troubled me, especially for kids so young. Where did they pick up these divisive traits? But as they sat with me and we slowly worked out the tangled root of their troubles, I decided to settle in for a long conversation. It was a moment for a layer to be added, an opportunity to make a bridge toward a better path forward. Perhaps it wasn't significant enough for them to remember in the long run. But who knows, it could be a layer that led to a kinder, gentler character that might one day become a great missionary, a skilled surgeon, or just a basketball coach. God doesn't distinguish. Each in their own way builds the kingdom of God, which is startlingly accomplished by small acts of great love. And it is our prayer that the song being sung on the way out of our doors contain the steadfast words given by the One who is faithful to the end of time: *Noli timere.* Do not be afraid.

CHAPTER 23

BUILD YOUR PART

Then the Lord answered me and said: Write the vision;
make it plain on tablets, so that a runner may read it. For
there is still a vision for the appointed time; it speaks of the
end, and does not lie. If it seems to tarry, wait for it; it will
surely come, it will not delay. (Habakkuk 2:2–3)

The first formal teaching I had was in Sunday School as a five-year-old in a slanted-roof room on the top floor of my country church. My cousins and first friends gathered with our teacher there, and we learned a finger play about church. We locked our little hands together in such a way that our fingers were hidden inside our palms. And then:

Thumbs together: *Here is the church.* Pointer fingers slanted and touching: *Here is the steeple.* Spread apart hands: *Open the doors.…* Wiggle inside fingers: *See all the people.*

Simple. Profound. The church has a structure whose door is open to all. The building's highest point gestures to heaven and invites in the divine presence. But the living heart of it all, the wiggling breathing space, is the people. It was my first lesson, and it might have been the most important.

Decades later, I had my own group of six-year-olds gathered at my feet. I taught them that old finger play, and they spontaneously did what our little Sunday School group had done. At the end of the verse, they lifted their hands straight up, still locked together, fingers waving and dancing, the joyous people of the church.

I learned a lot of important life lessons in that prairie church about faith and community, about giving children roots and wings. Several miles down a grid road from our farm and then onto a rather bumpy, potholed highway was our tiny but vibrant country church. It was the church of my growing-up years, and those years were as formative in learning about education as any of my university classes that came later. In hindsight, foundational blocks were developing that would profoundly influence me later as I watched those adults around me as a kid, a teenager, and a university student.

In that space, all kids were church kids, and we found our place in an institution that preceded us by generations. The Russian Mennonite immigrants who settled on that prairie land chose first to build a church. Establishing a community of faith and a place of belonging was hugely important. That faith community was warm, nurturing, and foundational in the lives of those who began it and those who carried it on. Each played a different part, equally significant.

What I absorbed in the walls of that place was how important it was for a cause to be owned in all aspects. No task was too insignificant, and many hands made light and joyful work.

As teenagers, I remember my brother and I driving down that bumpy highway on our way home from a games night at our cousins. We noticed a light left on in an upstairs room of the church. Initially, we drove by. But we were barely past the driveway when, by mutual agreement, we turned around and went back to switch off the lights. We knew our parents wouldn't have driven by, and we shouldn't either because it was ours to look after. We were learning about ownership and commitment in small and large ways.

This richness of church life was in my bones and influenced my vision for Christian schooling. When I first walked into our school, I joined something already familiar. In my heart and soul, I rejoiced. I had found a place where people welcomed and embraced you, whether you were a Kindergarten kid starting out or an alumnus coming back for a visit. This was a place where lots of people needed to be committed to the cause of Christian education. It was vitally important for raising our children that the school joined together with the family and the church. It was a place where, through countless fundraising events, sports tournaments, musicals, class activities, facility moves, and run-of-the-mill tasks—many hands made light and joyful work—lifelong friendships for children and adults were formed. It was a place where God's Word was studied and committed to heart. It was a slice of God's kingdom invested in by many before me and by many after. My piece was small. The faithfulness of many was large. We each played our part as best we could.

In the final chapters of Joshua, we read Joshua's dying words. His farewell address to the tribes of Israel is given just before his death. He speaks the words of the Lord, explaining not only what transpired in his life but also a long sweep of their ancestors. He recounted their roots of faith. And those roots were deep. I love the version that begins as a story:

> Long ago your ancestors—Terah and his sons Abraham and Nahor—lived beyond the Euphrates and served other gods. Then I took your father Abraham from beyond the River and led them through all the land of Canaan and made his offspring many. I gave him Isaac; and to Isaac I gave Jacob and Esau. I gave Esau the hill country to Seir to possess, but Jacob and his children went down to Egypt.... (Joshua 24: 2–4)

He carried on with his discourse, and it is all familiar. We've heard it before, and we know how the story continues. We know that there is still much between these lines that Joshua doesn't recount. What's important is telling the story, passing on to the next generation the memory of the past. Like children, we rarely tire of the retelling. And most significantly, there is a Giver in this story. Notice how God says in the story: *I gave him Isaac. I gave Jacob and Esau. I gave Esau the hill country.* There is a Giver, and the story is about a gift and the people taking that gift. They didn't always use the gifts wisely. There are lots of faults and flaws in God's people, but in God's time, the work is done one generation at a time. In generation after generation, God worked the impossible at the last moment, in the fullness of time. He gave an heir and created a future for Sarah, Rebekah, and Rachel when none seemed available. To

Elizabeth and Mary. It is an astonishing legacy of intervention by the Great I Am.

These are the stories and themes we need to pass on to our children. We also need to continue this story to include their place in it. We need to keep repeating that story because the past creates the context for the present and the future. While the greatest treasure of my life is the people of God's kingdom, I have to say a great blessing of my school years was seeing the long game, the story of a wandering school unfolding to a place of permanence. Through multiple school locations that were run down, temporary steps on the journey, where basic survival was always an issue, we clung to the story of the Israelites wandering and eventually reaching the Promised Land. For our school, it took seventeen years before the land was secured and ours. And we built a permanent home in an astonishing 128 days from groundbreaking. It took many, many committed people who prayed, gave what they could, volunteered endlessly, negotiated at city hall, built a beautiful structure, and moved all our bits and pieces for the final, glorious time.

The first day of school came when the school community gathered in the new atrium in an almost finished school, and we knew among the first things we needed to do was to give thanks and sing praise. So I stood on a temporary, incomplete stage and offered thanks. When I lifted my head and stepped back from the podium so that a teacher could lead the children in song, I was transfixed by the moment: the entire atrium and each person there was bathed in brilliant sunlight and God's radiant love. When I heard those children's voices sweetly sing, the sound rose through the doors, through the steeple, to God in heaven. I was overcome with the enormity and holiness of the moment. This was an acknowledgement of the faithfulness of the past, the beauty of this precise moment, the potential for the future I wouldn't see. I stepped off that stage fully aware of the fullness of God's timing, and tears slipped silently. There was no singing past the lump in my throat. A wise, long-time school supporter saw what was going on and enfolded me in his arms. I regained my composure in his warm embrace.

Sometimes it seems like a long wait to see God's plan put in action. Like Joseph, we may experience estrangement and despair before glory and power. Like the disciples, we may blunder and ask the wrong questions along the way. Or, like Moses, who persevered so long and faithfully with God's people, we may never see the fruit of our labours, the reason for our toil, or the outcome of our agonized steps. We may only get a small section of the whole story in our lifetime, but it is a section we are called to be faithful in before passing it on to others who will carry the torch next.

Psalm 90 says, *"For a thousand years in thy sight are but as yesterday when it is past, or like a watch in the night"* (Psalm 90:4). Part of our responsibility to our children is to help them see that they are included in the story thousands of years in the making so that they can plant roots and grow to be faithful servants in God's kingdom. Their road may be crooked with trying sections. But we can give them a lantern to carry on the way—a defining and holy vision of sacred purpose for the place that is their section of road to build. And we can nurture in them a spark of hope to carry out of our doors. As Anne Lamott writes, "Hope begins in the dark; the stubborn hope that if you just show up and try to do the right thing, the dawn will come. You wait and watch and work—you don't give up."[9]

A vision of eternal light. A spark of hope. These are the tools for each of us to carry close to our hearts for a life of purpose. There is much to accomplish in kingdom building. Our lives are a promise to God to keep spreading his news. The journey has richness, beauty, and purpose. The people beside us are wiggling in their vibrancy. We build God's kingdom and pass on that torch so that the story continues, even unto the ends of the earth.

The path is holy ground, which can be realized from the first moment little fingers are clasped together, and the story of God's people begins afresh. Together, God's kingdom is built by those whose past faithfulness was carried on by sparks of the future. It is realized in the fullness of God's endless and magnificent time.

Build your part as you have been called. May our roots be deep as we accept the gift from the Giver of all life. And let us live in the

---

[9] Anne Lamott, *Bird by Bird: Some Instructions on Writing and Life* (Anchor, 1995), 27.

awareness that each moment given to us is utterly and simply sacred in all of the ordinary days of our lives.

THE STORIES ARE THE LAST TO GO

Recently, I was once again driving on that straight road that is the ribbon between my two worlds: the prairie of my home province and the distant city that drew me away. To help pass the time, my radio was tuned to CBC, where I heard a familiar voice: Robert Munsch was speaking to host Sheilagh Rogers on *The Next Chapter* in his first interview in a decade.[10] His voice wasn't as strong as it once was, but it was still easy to recognize. The famed storyteller had entertained endlessly, speaking from a much-worn tape in my classroom while my Grade ones painted their masterpieces. I'm pretty sure the art exploding from the tape influenced the art on the paper.

You couldn't be a Grade one teacher in Canada without immersing yourself in Robert Munch's stories. I had an entire language-arts theme built on his work, and there were many after-recess–story-times when the students handed me their book of choice. It was Robert Munsch's work. They happily called out the repetitive lines, laughed at the same parts every time, and sang along to "I'll love you forever." They cheered every time the Paper Bag Princess did *not* marry the prince and collectively ducked so the Mud Puddle wouldn't land on them.

In one of my early years at our school, we entered a nationwide contest to sell Robert Munsch's calendars filled with illustrations and text from his books. The Canadian school that sold the most calendars

---

[10] "The Next Chapter," Hosted by Sheilagh Rogers, CBC Radio, October 1, 2021.

received a day-long visit from the storyteller himself. Our small school didn't have a population that would benefit us in this contest, but we were good at fundraising, and our families and kids got right at it and sold a bunch of calendars. In retrospect, I'm pretty sure the financial gain was minimal, but every penny mattered in those years. So you can imagine our shock when we won the contest. From every participating school in Canada, our school sold the most calendars. We anticipated our reward.

The excitement was palpable on the day Mr. Munsch was to arrive. He had plans to visit every classroom and then end the day with a school assembly. I vaguely wondered what he would think of flying from Ontario to this rundown school, but I shouldn't have worried. There was no pretense in this famous storyteller—only kindness and a genuine interest in being with children. Munsch got his energy off of kids, and after he shed his coat, he sat down in my Grade one class. With my students in rapt attention at his knees, he got about the business of telling stories. They weren't just the tried-and-true ones—although he didn't disappoint in that area. He also gave the kids a lesson in how to write stories. He asked if they would like to tell a story with him, and he drew out of them a setting, some characters, and a story problem. In no time at all, they made up a new story. He told them that he often practiced stories out loud first before writing them down, and maybe one day the story they had just invented might be in a book. They beamed at him. For now, they were also storytellers.

At the final assembly, we had an all-school surprise for Munsch. I had taken snippets from Munsch's books and compiled a thank you story for him, incorporating sections from each book. Every class was given a different segment of the story, and when their part came up, they chorused their lines before volleying the next section of the story over to student narrators in the next class. They were well-rehearsed, so I was able to sit back and absorb the scene. I carefully watched Munsch's face. He couldn't stop smiling, enthralled as his words came back to him in new ways. Most of all, he was so pleased with the combined energy of the students in front of him who took such delight in surprising him. It was a sparkling moment.

The voice now on my radio while I drove that straight road still had some of that spark. Munsch couldn't help being dramatic even in "just an interview," and he drew out words and played with sounds.

But it was an older voice now, facing a difficult dementia diagnosis. When the interviewer asked him what the future held, he honestly replied that it wasn't good—he would eventually be in a dementia ward somewhere. "But," she pressed, "you still remember the stories." "Yes," he said, "the stories will be the last to go."

I had to grip my wheel a bit because my view was suddenly blurry. I had just spent many months remembering stories. I thought of all the lonely hours in the recent too-long pandemic days as people around the world sat alone and isolated. While much was taken away, what didn't leave us were our stories—those of the past, those spinning on the airwaves, those we were imagining for the future. Jesus knew that stories captivated people, and they were his main medium for spreading his message. A story encapsulated what was important to say without beating the message into someone. A story links people throughout the world, providing a sense of belonging and pointing to tidbits of wisdom.

I can't get the final picture that Robert Munsch painted of himself out of my mind. I imagine him in his quiet room, without the laughter and energy of children. It's sad to me as I understand that absence. But then I look closer, and I see what's in his heart and mind. It's not sad; it's joyous. It's story after story, accompanied by the spellbound faces and laughter of countless children, illuminated in countless schools he entered, to share countless words. Stories were his timeless gift to share with the world, and these are also ours to give each other with the images that are still vibrant and alive in our hearts.

This is the end of my school stories. There are more vowels, consonants, and properly placed apostrophes drifting along the horizon that will eventually form new words and images. But don't let the end of this particular storybook stop you. Pull a child onto your lap, gather your family around the table, lean over your neighbour's fence, and tell your stories.

Because the stories will be the last to go.

Shalom, my friends.

ACKNOWLEDGEMENTS

When I was three, I borrowed my dad's special blue pen. He kept it in the cupboard, hanging on a plastic spray-painted Father's Day trophy my brother had made him. I took that coveted writing piece into the living room, hid behind the long curtains, and wrote carefully in neat zigzags a long, stirring, and undecipherable piece... onto the wall. It was my first foray into writing. It was exhilarating, sneaky, and it earned me the only two spankings I ever got. My first writing had to be painted over to be extinguished, but the muse never left. I didn't realize until this past year that the muse disrupts you. I could lie awake until 3:00 a.m. figuring out a tricky story part and then wake up four hours later, tired and sleep-deprived but still organizing the words to find their proper home. And by the way, the Peace Officer whose job it is to write tickets—not stories—doesn't care if you are so absorbed about the words in your book that you unwittingly blow by the reduced speed limit.

I need to thank my lovely mother, Katie Wiens, who found ways to redirect those early scribbles. She provided me with more legitimate instruments—paper, pencil, envelopes and stamps—and I was sending off stories to the *Western Producer* children's writing section by elementary school. She kept those badly written stories and decades later added all 130 editorials I wrote for our school newsletter to the file, which were seed stories for this book. Such is a mother's love. My mom consistently showed me that writing meaningful notes to people is a form of ministry—as important to kingdom building as a Sunday sermon. I have a long way to go before catching up to her note-writing output.

The teacher in me wants to underscore the importance of modelling reading and writing for our children. My Opa, Peter B. Wiens, left our farm just about when I was writing zigzags on the wall to become the editor of the German church paper, *Der Bote*. When we visited in my grandparents' new home—no longer across the hedgerow from us—our Oma frequently shooed us into the living room away from the study with the words, "Play quietly, Opa is writing his editorial." And so my brother and I were quiet for what seemed like interminable hours until our Opa finally emerged, ready to take us on a walk to the train bridge. If we were lucky, a train came rattling by while we were standing on the pedestrian side, rollicking the entire structure and just maybe finally clearing the words from his head. When I saw Opa's editorials years later, they weren't that long. But I knew from the time he put into them that each word was crafted with care. After all, pen and paper meant he couldn't hit the delete key! When I wrote my editorials decades later, I often thought of him sitting in his orange chair with pen and paper, thinking and thinking about his words. If even a little bit of that creativity leaked through the generations to me, I am honoured and grateful for his example. Please model reading and writing to your children and grandchildren so they can journey into the delightful world of imagination and develop their own creations.

For over two decades, I walked alongside some of the nicest people this side of heaven. The Menno community was a happy, energizing, and warm place to land. I am grateful for the teachers and staff members. They did the hard work of implementing our vision in the daily, minute-by-minute muck of life. I stood at the door and greeted people, and it was with immense pride and love that I watched from this vantage point as they got to work each day. The families who joined us soon realized that a school just starting required lots of extra work; and the contributions of time, commitment, and passion from these wonderful people was inspiring.

Of course, the kids were the reason we were there. Those Menno kids wormed their way into our hearts and were the reason we wakened with eternal purpose each day. I'm grateful for them all.

Special mention goes to Ruth Esau, who pulled me into her writing world by asking me to edit her leadership books and then graciously pushed me into my own pieces. It was at a writing retreat with her that author Mark Buchanan's opening words jolted my heart. He said that it wasn't a writer's job to decide if the world needed another book, but it was their job to be faithful to the inspiration of the Holy Spirit. And so, this book lurched into being.

Writing is a solitary endeavour; publishing is teamwork. Word Alive Press honoured me by placing my early manuscript on their longlist for the Braun Book Awards. It was a small and giant final push to give my words flight. Thanks to project manager Marina Reis for expertly guiding me through the publishing process and to Rick Johnson whose editing made this a better book.

And finally, to the One who calls each of us Beloved, be all honour, glory, and praise. Walk in his light.